MW00608012

The Knights Templar

A Captivating Guide to a Powerful Catholic Military Order and Their Impact on the Crusades

Free Bonus from Captivating History (Available for a Limited time)

Hi History Lovers!

Now you have a chance to join our exclusive history list so you can get your first history ebook for free as well as discounts and a potential to get more history books for free! Simply visit the link below to join.

Captivatinghistory.com/ebook

Also, make sure to follow us on Facebook, Twitter and Youtube by searching for Captivating History.

Youtube: Captivating History

Table of Contents

Introduction

In 1819, Sir Walter Scott wrote and published one of his best historical novels, *Ivanhoe.* In its pages, we are introduced to memorable characters, such as the protagonist Wilfred of Ivanhoe, his love interest, Lady Rowena, and Rebecca of York. A significant character in the book is Brian de Bois-Guilbert, a member of the Order of the Knights Templar. Sir Brian is an introduction for many people to the most prominent order of knights in medieval Europe.

Officially known as the Poor Fellow-Soldiers of Christ and of the Temple of Solomon, the Templars' story is an epic comprised of facts and legends. They were known for their fighting skill, but they also were financial professionals whose innovations in international commerce and banking are still used today. They were fierce warriors who defended the Christian holdings in Palestine but were ultimately destroyed by a Christian king who wanted their money.

The Knights Templar was a product of the Crusades. Committed to protecting pilgrims on their sojourns to holy sites in the Middle East, everything the Templars did was to serve that goal. Theirs is a fantastic story of combat, money, and mystery. The Templar Order continues to excite the imagination of people, even though the Templars were wiped out in the 14th century.

This book is dedicated to the story of the Knights Templar and the path the knights rode through the Middle Ages. Heroes and villains, saints and sinners, and ordinary men could be found in the ranks at any given time during the order's existence. Their tale is fascinating and provides an understanding of the roots of modern banking, which are planted firmly in the legacy of the Templars.

We will be exploring several facets of the order. This book will investigate the Templars' origins, battlefield exploits, and diplomacy as they defended Outremer from Muslim adversaries. In addition, we will look at the financial institutions that were created to support its military operations and the kangaroo court atmosphere of the final demise of the Knights Templar.

We must recognize the legends and myths of this band of fighting monks, and we will look at some of the more extraordinary folktales. Our goal is to acquaint you with an organization whose numbers were rarely over twenty thousand but whose presence significantly influenced European history between the 12th and 14th centuries.

Chapter One –Outremer

"On the eighth day after the city was taken they chose Duke Godfrey as its ruler, so that he might fight against the pagans and protect the Christians."

-Gesta Francorum, 1962

On July 15th, 1099, a European army performed the improbable but not the impossible. That was the day Crusaders broke through the walls of Jerusalem and captured the city. The Crusaders were running out of water, and a Fatimid relief army was coming up from Egypt. It seemed unlikely that the Crusaders would be able to take the city, but they did, and their success changed the political landscape of the Middle East.

The Outremer Empire

The Crusader States were finalized as political entities shortly after the capture of Jerusalem. These states included the County of Edessa, the Principality of Antioch, the County of Tripoli, and the Kingdom of Jerusalem. The initial rulers were all leaders of the First Crusade: Baldwin of Boulogne (Edessa), Bohemond Taranto (Antioch), Raymond of Toulouse (Tripoli), and Godfrey of Bouillon (Jerusalem). The now Christian-controlled area was referred to as the Crusader States or Outremer, which is French for "overseas."

The newly formed Christian States would significantly influence affairs in the Middle East until 1291, when the final Christian stronghold, Acre, fell. The effect the Crusader States had on the West, especially on international trade in the Mediterranean, was staggering. Thus, the fall of

Jerusalem in 1099 offered an enormous opportunity for everyone living in Europe.

The Economic Significance of Outremer

The First Crusade was originally launched to take Jerusalem and to open pilgrimage routes to the holy places in the Middle East. Jerusalem had been besieged and taken many times before, with the Fatimids taking it in 1098 after it had been controlled by the Seljuk Turks since 1073.

We sometimes forget that this area of the world was a major economic center where commerce flourished. The Crusader States were not comprised of vast farmlands. It was a highly urbanized part of the Mediterranean, with major economic centers scattered throughout the territory. The Christians controlled the primary ports, including Beirut, Tyre, Antioch, Jaffa, and Ascalon. Commodities, such as incense, gold, silver, and ivory, passed through these cities to Europe and elsewhere. While these trade items came through the Crusader States from other places, Outremer also had export items that included sugar, religious souvenirs, leather goods, pottery, and other crafts.[1]

The Crusader States were the doorway to Europe, and demand for various products rose dramatically in the West. People in Europe were introduced to spices and other exotic goods they had never known before, and once they got a taste for them, the craving for these new flavors never left their palate. Outremer was not some vast desert or treeless plain. It was a place where people could make their fortunes, and many Europeans chose to try their luck in the marketplace of Jerusalem and Caesarea. It was a time of economic opportunity and market exploration that was only equaled when Christopher Columbus set sail in 1492.

There is much to say about the economic benefits of Outremer, but there was a caveat. This region of the world held some severe disadvantages. To put it bluntly, it was a prosperous place, but it was not a safe place for Christians. The risks were high and dangerous.

---

[1] The Crusader Kingdoms. (2023, January 30). *Luxury Exports and Religious Tourist: The Urban Economy of Outremer*. Retrieved from www.crusaderkingdoms.com : https://www.crusaderkingdoms.com/urban-economy.html

The Vulnerability of Outremer

The Islamic world was shocked by the fall of Jerusalem in 1099, and the impact of the Crusaders' success was felt almost immediately in the shops and bazaars of Muslim communities. Muslim merchants now had to deal with Christian trade practices and fees that the new rulers charged for doing business in what was once their backyard. It was a development that none of them cared for, and a return to the pre-Crusade days was desired.

The Crusader States were conquered by force of arms. Now, the lands the Crusaders had taken had to be held by those same soldiers who won the territory. That was not going to be a simple task to perform. The Christians were surrounded on three sides by Muslim populations who did not care for the presence of nonbelievers in their midst. Internal squabbling in the Muslim world hampered an immediate counterattack. Still, it was just a matter of time before the Western interlopers were to be challenged for their lands in the Levant.

There was no guarantee that the original Crusader unity was going to last. Each ruler of the Crusader States had their own needs and their own ideas for policy. There were going to be disagreements, and any break in their solidarity was an opportunity for Muslim leaders to step in and retake lost lands, realizing a substantial increase in profit as a result.

The Crusader lords could not count on the loyalty of their new subjects. These people would accept their new rulers only for as long as it benefited them and didn't upset their daily activities. It would not be difficult to stir up the population against their new masters, so the new powers always had to be vigilant. Volunteers from France and other Western countries were available, but these were primarily freebooters and were the cause of as much trouble as any raider from Egypt or Syria. The situation was shaky at best and dangerous at worst.

What was needed was a military force that transcended the borders that had been recently created. Christians in Outremer needed a group of fighting men that was dedicated to maintaining Christianity in the area and that had the military prowess to beat back a much larger Muslim opponent. These same warriors had to commit to protecting the pilgrims and maintaining the new status quo.

They needed to be selfless men who were prepared to die in the course of achieving their mission. In addition, this independent police force would need the financial resources to pay for the equipment and upkeep of a mobile force in an unforgiving climate. That was a lot to ask of anyone. It was a question of security that needed to be addressed from the very beginning.

Approximately twenty years after the fall of Jerusalem, a solution to this problem came galloping out of the West.

Chapter Two – The Early Days

"The warriors are gentler than lambs and fiercer than lions, wedding the mildness of the monk with the valor of the knight, so that it is difficult to decide which to call them."

-Bernard of Clairvaux

Western Europe faced a sizable social problem in the late 11th century. However, the trouble did not come from the peasants or the townspeople. Instead, the nobility, the ruling class, faced an issue that needed to be addressed. Failure to do so could result in violent and bloody consequences.

The rule of inheritance was primogeniture. The eldest son got the title and the property, leaving younger sons to figure out a way to make a living and earn income. Unfortunately, medieval society severely limited the possible choices for younger siblings.

Embracing a religious life was one option. The Roman Catholic Church was the largest bureaucracy in the Western world at the time. There were opportunities if a young nobleman wanted to take advantage of them. It did not mean they would be parish priests. Instead, their families would view the church as a place where an intelligent boy could eventually rise to become a bishop, an abbot, or even the pope. Those positions would enable a family to gain influence and necessary favors from the church hierarchy. The path least taken was for an adolescent from an aristocratic family to become an upper-level bureaucrat in some diocese. That would not be a bad place to end up at all.

The other option was more dangerous to society. Young men with a blue-blooded lineage may have been taught how to read, write, and understand Latin, but they were usually not bookworms. However, they were also trained in the military arts and became very proficient in horseback riding and the use of various weapons. To put it bluntly, they were trained to kill. Younger sons could join up with a mercenary band or become a vassal to a king or noble. Their primary function was to be ready to wage war and do so ruthlessly.

The Norman conquest of England in 1066 and the First Crusade, which lasted from 1096 to 1099, allowed young aristocrats to use their military knowledge to their advantage. Their looting and pillaging did not affect mainland Europe. Still, there were many well-trained young men in armor who needed to be kept busy doing something other than burning down small villages in domestic feuds or freebooting escapades.

There had to be some way younger sons could either make the best of their military skills or have a place in a bureaucracy that would employ their intellectual talents. An appealing cause would ensure they remained loyal. And a philosophy or motivation that transcended their everyday life and gave them meaning and purpose could direct them toward a higher good that would improve society instead of wrecking it.

A French knight named Hugues de Payens had a solution that would combine religious inclinations and military skills to attract young men who otherwise would be busy stealing their neighbors' cattle.

The First Grand Master

What we know of Hugues de Payens is that he was a knight from the Champagne region of France and that he was born around 1070. He may have served in the First Crusade under Godfrey of Bouillon. There is reason to believe that he was familiar with the Holy Land and may have gone on pilgrimage there after the First Crusade.

The pilgrim trade was ramping up in the early 12th century, but there were some serious obstacles. Pilgrims were being attacked repeatedly by brigands, and traveling to the holy sites was dangerous. Hugues de Payens felt something had to be done about it, and the solution required more than prayers. His idea was to have an order of knights or trained warriors who would take holy vows, including poverty, chastity, and obedience. They would be committed to the service of God. They would be considered warrior monks, men who had a military background and deep religious faith. The original name of this group was the Poor

Fellow-Soldiers of Christ and of the Temple of Solomon.

According to the Archbishop William of Tyre, the first chronicler of the Knights Templar, the order was formed in 1118 by de Payens and his associate, Godfrey de. St Omer.[2] The original group consisted of nine knights of noble rank. The group approached the king of Jerusalem, Baldwin II, and told him of their desire to defend pilgrims from the Muslims and other dangers that faced them on their journey. Baldwin gave the knights temporary quarters in the palace.

It was not easy to get recruits, and the Knights Templar ran into financial difficulties. The order was sworn to poverty, but as a fighting unit, they needed funds to carry out their mission. They also required recruits. Europe was the ideal place to get both money and men. Fortunately for the order, one of the members, André de Montbard, had a famous relative who would prove to be the greatest advocate for the Knights Templar in their early days.[3]

The Last of the Fathers

The Late Middle Ages produced giants of Christian theology. Men such as Thomas Aquinas, Duns Scotus, William of Occam, and Bonaventure provided richness to the study of theology, influencing thinkers centuries after they passed away. One of the titans of God in this era was Bernard of Clairvaux. His writing and preaching left such an impression during his life and afterward that he was canonized by the Roman Catholic Church on January 18th, 1174, and would later be declared a doctor of the church.[4]

Bernard was born in 1090 and came from Burgundian aristocracy. Bernard entered a monastic community in Citeaux in 1112 and founded an abbey at Clairvaux in 1115. He became well known as a theological writer while he was the abbot of the Cistercian abbey at Clairvaux and composed considerable works of theology during his tenure. Bernard was sought out by popes and kings for his advice. He was very well connected, and his word was taken as gospel by many of the intellectuals of his time. Bernard was the nephew of André de Montbard.

---

[2] Templar History. (2020, June 7). *Hugues de Payens-The First Grand Master.* Retrieved from https://templarhistory.com : https://templarhistory.com/hugues-de-payens-the-first-grand-master/

[3] Templar History. (2020, June 7). *Hugues de Payens-The First Grand Master.*

[4] Meyer, J. R. (2023, January 1). *St. Bernard of Clairvaux.* Retrieved from www.Britannica.com: https://www.britannica.com/biography/Saint-Bernard-of-Clairvaux

Relationship with the Templars

The association between Bernard of Clairvaux and the Knights Templar no doubt sprouted from Bernard's family contact with one of the original knights. Bernard was impressed with the goals and objectives of the order and became an official sponsor of the Templars. His patronage was a substantial boost to a knightly order that was struggling.

Bernard had more than kind thoughts about these warrior monks. He became a powerful advocate for the Templars, and the knights figured prominently in Bernard's work, *In Praise of the New Knighthood.* Bernard used his considerable influence in ecclesiastical circles to convince the pope to officially recognize the Order of the Templars. This was done at the Council of Troyes in 1129. The contact with the pope went further when Pope Innocent II, who was once a monk at Clairvaux, authorized the first papal donation of money to the Templars.

An even more fantastic present to the Templars from Innocent II came in the papal bull *Omne datum optimum,* which was published in 1139. This decree exempted the Templars from local taxes. Furthermore, the Templars were able to move throughout the world and answered to nobody but the pope himself.

This was an incredible boon. The Templars were now free from any restraints brought on by local rulers. The knights could operate in Christendom without fear of any censure from a local sovereign. It would prove to be very advantageous since the Templars performed other services in the Crusader States. Bernard's influence also boosted donations and gifts granted to the Templars by the ruling classes of Christian Europe.

The increasing notoriety of the Knights Templar drew recruits from everywhere. The order matured and became a force to be reckoned with in Outremer and western Europe. It rapidly became the preeminent knightly order of the Middle Ages.

The contributions of Bernard of Clairvaux went one step further. The Council of Troyes authorized him to create the Rule for the Templars. That was going to be the guide to all the actions of this order and the rules the knights were expected to follow for the rest of their days as defenders of Christian pilgrims.[5]

Bernard would go on to preach and advocate for the Second Crusade. While this crusade was not successful, it did not tarnish Bernard's reputation, as he became ever more influential. He would continue to be the most prominent of the Cistercian Order and would debate theology with opponents such as Abelard. His thoughts on theology influenced later scholars, and even Martin Luther was impressed by what Bernard of Clairvaux wrote.

The last honor that was given to this medieval monastic came in an encyclical written by Pope Pius XII and issued on May 24th, 1953 (long after Bernard's death). The pope referred to Bernard as "Doctor Mellifluus" and the "last of the Fathers." In other words, Bernard was the last of the great doctors of the church, placing him in the company of the greatest minds of Roman Catholic theology.

Bernard left one enduring gift to the Knights Templar: the Latin Rule, which governed all the activities of a Templar from the moment he rose in the morning to his last acts in the evening.

The Latin Rule

Medieval society was full of orders and associations of people brought together for various purposes. The monastic world assembled men of above-average intellect who shared a common space and lived their lives together as a community. These clusters needed to have some form of guidance in how to live their lives and manage daily affairs, which was why the monastic orders had written rules. The most prominent was the Rule of St. Benedict. Benedict of Nursia wrote it in the 6th century. The rule was used to regulate the life of the Benedictine Order, which was one of the most influential monastic groups in the Middle Ages.

Much has been written about the importance of monastic rules and their impact on the lives of those who followed them. We may think there is nothing comparable to these in our modern society. However, a closer inspection of the rules of various monastic orders shows that they have something in common with modern management. Frankly, works such as the Rule of St. Benedict are employee manuals intended to

---

[5] Electricscotland.com. (2023, January 31). *Bernard of Clairvaux: Patron Saint of the Templar Order*. Retrieved from https://www.electricscotland.com/: https://www.electricscotland.com/books/ries/BERNARD%20OF%20CLAIRVAUX%20011713.pdf.

impress on people the importance of various activities and teach each member the group's mission.

If a person glances through some of these texts, they will discover that there are periods of time each day set aside for recreation, reflection, and daily work to sustain the monastery. There were dietary rules, but only the strictest orders insisted on near starvation. The right kind of nutrition was expected to be followed.

With the idea that what a Templar followed and obeyed can be thought of as a knight's employee manual for his career, we can investigate the precepts that distinguished a Templar from other medieval associations.

The Origins of the Latin Rule

The Latin Rule was commissioned by the Council of Troyes, which met in 1129 to consider issues that concerned the Order of the Knights Templar. The first grand master of the Templars, Hugues de Payens, requested that a rule be established for the Templars. Bernard of Clairvaux, who convened the council, was commissioned to write it. He would be aided by Hugues de Payens in its composition. The final copy is referred to as the Latin Rule.

The Latin Rule drew inspiration from the Rule of St. Benedict and the Rule of St. Augustine. It started with seventy-two rules, but this would be expanded to several hundred. What the Templars followed was different than other rules created at that time. Monastic orders were essentially scholarly groups deeply devoted to meditation and reflection. The Templars were essentially fighters. They would not be busy copying sacred and classical texts in the scriptorium.

The Templars were going to be on the battlelines, defending pilgrims and fighting Muslim armies. Consequently, the Latin Rule combined religious contemplation with battle orders and made modifications to fasting rules so that it would not impede a Templar in combat.

The Latin Rule has admonitions that we may think of as idiosyncratic. However, these were very serious instructions to keep the Knights Templar focused on their mission and have the necessary physical and psychological tools to become exceptional warriors.

The Quirks

The Templars followed tenets that, to a modern audience, appear strange and even downright funny. It is essential to recognize that rules of various orders in the Middle Ages had different connotations back then, so what we think is strange was perfectly acceptable and reasonable at that time. Any rule of a monastic order was intended to set them apart from society at large. The Knights Templar was no different than those who lived in monasteries devoted to chanting hymns and copying books. Nevertheless, some of their strange rules deserve comments.

1. Templars were not to have physical contact with their own families.

   This rule meant that once a young man entered the order, there would be no more association with the family he came from. The Templar knights were drawn from the aristocracy, not the peasantry or the townspeople. The knights were related to some very powerful people who had their own interests. By keeping members away from their families, the order cemented the idea that Templars worked for the glory of God, not the advancement of their kin.

2. The knights were required to eat their meals in total silence.

   It wasn't out of the ordinary to insist on this rule. Other religious groups had the same restriction. However, it did not mean that nobody could talk in the dining hall. There would be somebody present who would read from scripture or some other religious text to the knights. Mealtime was a period when the body and mind were nourished. Templars probably developed a kind of sign language to understand specific requests at the table, such as passing the salt.

3. Templar knights were required to wear their white mantle at all times, even when eating, and they could not eat if they were not wearing their white mantle.

   The white mantle was more than just recognition of their brand; it symbolized an even closer connection to the order. The knights were to be committed to their mission, and constantly wearing the uniform, even when eating, reinforced the notion that being a Templar was not an ordinary job but a lifetime commitment.

4. Templars could only eat meat three times a week.

   Modern meals usually include a serving of meat. That was out of the ordinary in the Middle Ages when many people survived on porridge, vegetables, and some fruit. Meat was a luxury. Other religious orders denied members the ability to have meat at all.

However, meat was seen as being part of a weekly diet for a fighting man. The protein was necessary because of the military duties they were required to perform. So, the Templars allowed for meat even though other religious groups did not, which is comparable to the Muslim exemption from the Ramadan fast for those who were involved in holy wars against the infidels.[6]

5. Knights were prohibited from wearing pointed shoes and shoelaces.

   Recruits were drawn from the aristocracy, where flamboyant dress and style were part of the everyday experience. The Templars wanted none of that. Instead, a Templar was expected to concentrate on the mission and not worry about how they looked. Several regulations expressly address the idea of extravagant clothing. Allowances were made for the intense heat in Palestine, as linen shirts were permitted to the Templars stationed there.

Moving away from these warnings, there were serious martial guidelines for this military order. A chain of command was established, where the grand master had overall authority, a seneschal carried the battle standard, and a marshal issued battle equipment. The knights were organized into squadrons with their own knight commander and banner. Unquestioned obedience was the norm for a Templar. There was no concept of independent honor. This unquestioned discipline would serve the knights well since they held ranks longer than ordinary soldiers and moved as a unit instead of a mob.[7]

The Templars' commitment to the standard made them highly effective as a fighting unit. The Knights Templar were forbidden to surrender unless their flag had fallen. Moreover, they could not leave the battlefield until all the Templar flags had fallen. These soldiers of God were expected to keep fighting when ordinary knights would leave the field. Their willingness to do this was molded by adherence to the Latin Rule, even in the minor things of everyday life. The Latin Rule created a

---

[6] Medieval Chronicles.com. (2023, February 1). *8 Strange Rules Templar Knights Had to Obey?* Retrieved from https://www.medievalchronicles.com/: https://www.medievalchronicles.com/the-crusades/knights-templar/knights-templar-and-the-latin-rule/

[7] Howe, J. (2016, November/December). *Benard's Chosen: The Knights Templar.* Retrieved from http://myweb.ttu.edu/: http://myweb.ttu.edu/jhowe/syllabi/Templar%20Rule.pdf.

very professional fighting force.

The Latin Rule firmly impressed the brand of the order into its members' minds. The nuances and proclamations of the Latin Rule caused the Templars to stand out among other military associations. Moreover, the practices the Templars followed in adherence to the Latin Rule prepared them for the role they would play in the Crusades of the 12th century.

Chapter Three – Templars in Action: The Second Crusade

"I opened my mouth; I spoke; and at once the Crusaders have multiplied to infinity."

-Bernard of Clairvaux

The acceptance of the Templars at the Council of Troyes and the enthusiastic patronage of Bernard of Clairvaux were godsends to the young order. Recruiting became easy, as the Templars gained notoriety and young nobles flocked to join. In addition, donations and gifts to the Templars assured they would no longer be "Poor Knights." Instead, they would have the resources necessary to be a fully-fledged fighting force. The military capabilities of the warrior monks would be proven in the Second Crusade.

Origins of the New Crusade

The Muslims lost Jerusalem and the eastern Mediterranean coastline, but that did not mean they were giving up. On the contrary, they looked for any opportunity to contest the suzerainty of their unwelcome Christian neighbors, and the first chance came in the County of Edessa. The Seljuk leader Zengi took back Edessa in 1144. This capture signaled to western Europe that the Levant only belonged to the Christians if they were willing to fight hard to keep it.

Pope Eugenius III called for the Second Crusade, and Bernard of Clairvaux became the most enthusiastic advocate for military action.

Bernard was also an effective recruiter. He convinced King Conrad III of Germany and King Louis VII of France to participate in the campaign. The backing of these two mighty monarchs should have made the Second Crusade as successful as the first one. That did not happen.

The Second Crusade was a calamity of poor coordination. Conrad's contingent started early without any sense of organization or military discipline. Their relations with other Christians as they moved eastward were so bad that there were frequent skirmishes with the troops of the Byzantine Empire. The Germans' participation in the Second Crusade effectively ended in a disastrous defeat at Dorylaeum.

The French realized they could only get to the Middle East with the cooperation of the Byzantine Empire. Consequently, they sent envoys to the Byzantine emperor to negotiate the passage of the Crusaders through Byzantine territory. One of the envoys happened to be Everard de Barres, the Templar master in France who commanded three hundred Templars. The French diplomats were able to get the safe passage they needed.

The new crusading army moved carefully down the Mediterranean coast but was ambushed near Laodicea. The French survived the encounter but lost most of their horses and baggage train. Lacking any real military strategy, Louis gave command of his army to Everard de Barres, which was a brilliant decision.

De Barres instilled military command and discipline in the French ranks. The remaining French soldiers were organized into companies of fifty men, and these companies were placed under the command of a Templar. In addition, stability was created and maintained.

Templars gave very sensible instructions to their subordinates. The French men at arms were expected to protect the horses if the enemy attacked, and counterattacks were only to be attempted if they were adequately coordinated and led. Order was the rule of the day, and everyone was expected to follow instructions carefully. What happened to the Germans did not occur to the French, thanks to the oversight of the Templars.

Supplies ran scarce for the French but not for the Templars, who were careful with food distribution and fodder. The Templars could strike back at the Muslims and protect the entire army.

Unfortunately, all the efforts of the Knights Templar did not prevent the overall collapse of the Second Crusade. Bickering and finger-pointing destroyed the solidarity of the crusading army, and the force finally disintegrated. What started as a noble enterprise ended as a disorganized band of soldiers who fought more against each other than against their enemy[8].

Some recriminations were hurled against the Templars, but no one could deny that their strict military discipline allowed them to succeed when units of the crusading army faltered. The Templars next entered a period where significant physical proof of their existence dotted the region's landscape.

[8] Defenders of Jerusalem.com. (2023, February 2). *The Knights Templar Prove Their Mettle: The Second Crusade.* Retrieved from Defenders of Jerusalem.com: https://www.defenderofjerusalem.com/knights-templar---second-crusasde.html

Chapter Four – Templar Castles

"God sends his angels to Tortosa down, Godfrey unites Christian Peers and Knights; And all the Lords and Princes of renown."

-Torquato Tasso

The Templars began by living in borrowed space. The king of Jerusalem allowed them to live in one part of the royal palace, but he could evict them at any time. Things would dramatically change for the Templars in the span of just a few years.

With Bernard of Clairvaux advocating for them and the pope permitting the Templars to have an exemption from taxes, the Knights Templar was in a situation where it could dramatically increase its assets. The Second Crusade was a disaster but not necessarily for these warrior monks. They arguably prevented the French contingent from being annihilated, and their prestige was growing in Europe. Gifts and donations flooded into the order's coffers, which might have been embarrassing to a group of men who were sworn to poverty. What were they to do with all that cash?

If the donations were to be used for God's greater glory and the pilgrims' protection, the defense of the faithful was a serious option. The knights could create fortifications throughout Outremer where companies of the order might be stationed. Those same fortifications could be used as places for pilgrims to seek refuge and shelter.

That the Knights Templar were answerable only to the pope was likely aggravating to some of Outremer's ruling class because it put the order outside of their suzerainty. On the other hand, the Templars provided reliable security forces, and any defensive structure they built was a military obstacle that outside forces had to overcome. While there may have been some grumbling about the presence of an independent group of warriors, the rulers of the Crusader States had every reason to support the Knights Templar in establishing defensive positions throughout the area. During any time of relative peace in the 12th century, the order solidified its place in the Middle East.

In other words, the Knights Templar would go on a building spree. They built castles all over the region, which became the best defense against robbers and Muslim armies. The Templars certainly had the cash, thanks to all the donations given to them by the nobility of Europe, so they could afford to build the strongest castles in the world.

There are still remnants of them scattered throughout Palestine and Syria. However, they were not the wooden motte-and-bailey castles the Normans erected in England. Instead, the Templar castles were solid stone structures strategically located in areas that were easy to defend. These fortifications included high walls with round turrets, a large keep for protection, and open squares within the walls. The castle grounds might also contain substantial dry moats and multiple gatehouses for entrance control. It is an understatement to say that these castles were formidable structures.

The castles were also positions that could withstand lengthy sieges. That was an essential feature. A reasonably small garrison could defend a Templar castle. The grounds of the castle had sufficient storage areas where the garrison could store food and water that would last them for months. The defenders simply had to outlast the besieging force. The Templars could also use offensive measures, such as boiling oil to pour on besiegers and stakes planted in muddy areas to hinder riders from advancing on horseback.

Laying siege to a castle pinned down substantial numbers of troops who might be needed elsewhere to protect against uprisings or attacks from another Muslim principality.

Given the political instability of their enemies, the Knights Templar was able to build a series of castles in the 12th and 13th centuries that provided the protection that pilgrims needed and the practical defenses that Christian overlords required. Some of the Templar castles were magnificent, while others were smaller. However, there are several that can be considered outstanding examples.

Acre

Acre became the headquarters of the Knights Templar after the fall of Jerusalem. The main fortress of the Templars was established on the southwest side of the city. The Templar castle was protected by two great towers with twenty-eight-foot-thick walls. In addition, two smaller towers were built on either side of the main towers. An interesting feature of the fortress was a tunnel that measured over 490 feet. It extended to the city's port, which was located in the eastern part of Acre. The fall of Acre in 1291 signaled the end of the Crusader States.[9]

Tortosa

Tortosa was a hotly contested seaport and was originally a fiefdom of the County of Tripoli. Its location is near the Gate of Homs, a breach of the mountain ranges behind the coastal strip that made Tortosa a vital landing point for pilgrims headed to the Holy Land. The town exchanged hands several times but was eventually assigned to the Knights Templar.

The order built a citadel next to the harbor, and the town was completely fortified. The meeting hall of the citadel is still in existence, despite centuries of construction work. An interesting note about the citadel is that Saladin (the founder of the Ayyubid dynasty) was able to capture the town, but because he could not seize the citadel, he left Tortosa.[10]

Arwad

Arwad is the only inhabited island along the eastern coast of the Mediterranean. Its significance was serving as a staging point for expeditions into Outremer. In addition, Arwad was the final bastion of the Templars to fall to the Mamluks. It was intended to be a base from which Christians could reconquer the Crusader States in the 14th century. Instead, the Mamluks struck first and besieged Arwad, forcing it to surrender because it lacked food and water. What happened next was sheer treachery.

---

[9] Tourist Israel. (2023, February 10). *The Templar's Tunnel, Akko (Acre).* Retrieved from www.touristisrael.com: https://www.touristisrael.com/templars-tunnel-akko/28509/.

[10] My Travels in the Levant. (2023, February 10). *Tortosa and Arwad.* Retrieved from https://romeartlover.tripod.com: https://romeartlover.tripod.com/Tortosa.html

The Mamluks promised safe conduct to the defenders but reneged on the deal. They attacked the Templars as soon as the knights vacated the fortifications, killing the Templar leader, Barthélemy de Quincy, and either killing or enslaving most of the garrison. The surviving Templars were sent to a prison in Cairo.[11]

Château Pèlerin (Also Known as Atlit Castle)

Château Pèlerin is located on the northern coast of Israel, just south of Haifa. It was a powerful fortress and could support approximately four thousand troops if necessary. It was constructed in the 13th century to replace an earlier castle.

Château Pèlerin is an outstanding example of Crusader military architecture. It was built on a promontory, and the outer wall was approximately fifty feet high and twenty feet thick. Three square towers projected out thirty-nine feet and had level platforms on their roofs. The inner wall was taller than the outer wall so that defenders could shoot at targets coming over the first wall. Château Pèlerin had a protected harbor and three freshwater wells within its defenses. This castle dominated the north-to-south coastal road.

Château Pèlerin was never taken by a siege, primarily because its location allowed it to be resupplied by sea. The castle was finally abandoned shortly after the fall of Acre.

Temple Mount

Temple Mount was the Knights Templar headquarters until Jerusalem's fall in 1187. The Al Aqsa Mosque was commandeered by the Templars, who changed its name from the Dome of the Rock to the Templum Domini ("Temple of God"). The Templars enraged many Muslims by placing a gold cross on the top of the dome.

Despite this insult, the Templars enlarged the mosque and did not change the Arabic inscriptions inside the dome, even though the script denied the existence of the Trinity. The Templars did extensive excavations underneath the Temple Mount because they thought relics from the First Jewish Temple, including the Ark of the Covenant, might be found there. There is extensive tunnel work, and it includes

[11] Lebling, R. W. (2016, February 1). *Arwad, Fortress at Sea.* Retrieved from https://www.aramcoworld.com/: https://www.aramcoworld.com/Articles/January-2016/Arwad-Fortress-at-Sea

excavations near the Wailing Wall.[12]

Although the Knights Templar started its martial activity in the Levant, it did not restrict its efforts to that territory. The Knights Templar was also actively involved in Spain and Portugal during the Reconquista. As a result, there are several Templar castles located in those countries.

Peniscola Castle

Peniscola Castle was initially a Muslim fortification and was handed over to the king of Aragon in 1229. James II of Aragon gave the castle to the Templars in 1294, and the knights demolished what was left of the earlier defenses and completely rebuilt the castle. The castle was laid out with an inner ward and possessed a chapel. Other architectural features included barrel vaulting and round arches.

Tomar

Known as the Castelo dos Templarios, this castle was the most important Portuguese military fortification in the 12th century. Construction started on March 1st, 1160, and it was built to defend its borders with the Muslims. It remains one of the most prominent examples of defensive architecture in Portugal. The circular church within the grounds was modeled after the Dome of the Rock.[13]

Castle of San Servando

The castle was situated on a hill opposite Toledo, Spain. Castle of San Servando was a Visigothic monastery and was donated to the Knights Templar by King Alfonso VIII of Castile. The Templars rebuilt the castle to protect a bridge called Puente de Alcántara, which spans the gorge of the Tagus River.[14]

Castle of Almourol

The castle is on the islet of Almourol in the Tagus River. It was placed in the trust of the grand master of the Knights Templar in Portugal when it was captured in 1129. The Templars rebuilt it as part of

---

[12] McMahon, T. (2012, March 27). *Temple Mount-HQ of the Knights Templar.* Retrieved from thetemplarknight.com: https://thetemplarknight.com/2012/03/27/temple-mount-knights-templar/.

[13] https://www.portugaltravel.org/. (2023, February 10). *Castle of the Knights Templar in Tomar.* Retrieved from portugaltravel.org: https://www.portugaltravel.org/castle-of-the-knihgts-templar-tomar.

[14] Castles.nl. (2023, February 10). *San Servando Castle.* Retrieved from castles.nl: https://www.castles.nl/san-servando-castle.

the defensive line against the Muslims.

The Templars in the Iberian Peninsula and Outremer needed substantial amounts of money and supplies. There are Templar castles in Europe that were intended to be administrative and financial centers for the order. Here are some of the more important ones.

La Rochelle

A strong relationship between the La Rochelle and the Knights Templar existed almost from the beginning of the order. Eleanor of Aquitaine, the wife of King Henry II of England, exempted the Templars from duties and supported their activities.

It might sound incredible, but the Knights Templar, who we ordinarily would assume was land-based, had a fleet of ships, and La Rochelle was the most extensive Templar base on the Atlantic Ocean. The Templars were intermediaries in trade between England and the Mediterranean from this bustling seaport.

La Rochelle fits into the mythology of the Templars. A popular claim is that in 1307, a fleet of eighteen Templar ships set sail from La Rochelle to an unknown destination. Theorists speculate on where that flotilla of knightly boats ended up.[15]

Middle Temple

The Middle Temple was technically not a castle, but it was the headquarters of the Knights Templar in England. The Plantagenets were generous to the order and gave extensive land grants and privileges to the Templars. The knights acted less as warriors and more as bankers in London and worked as diplomats and advisors to the English kings. During the reign of Henry III, the Middle Temple became a significant oil administrative center. The area that was once Middle Temple is now a very prominent feature in the legal environment of London.[16]

---

[15] Ofteland. (2016, July 1). *La Rochelle-Atlantic Ocean Base for the Knights Templar*. Retrieved from discoversecretfrancecom.wordpress.com: https://discoversecretfrancedotcom.wordpress.com/2016/07/14/la-rochelle-atlantic-ocean-base-for-the-knights-templar/.

[16] Lyons, Z. (2023, February 11). *Temple Church and the Knights Templar*. Retrieved from layersoflondon.org: https://www.layersoflondon.org/map/records/temple-church-and-the-knights-templar.

Enclos du Temple

The Knights Templar was essentially a French order, so it made perfect sense for it to have its European headquarters in Paris. The castle no longer exists, but it was massive when it was still standing. The Templars were awarded a patch of marshland, which they dried out, and the area where the Templar headquarters once stood is still referred to as "le Marais."

What we know of the Enclos du Temple is that it had eight thirty-three-foot-high crenelated walls that were reinforced by turrets and buttresses. It once had a Gothic church, stables, and homes for the knights. It was not just an administrative headquarters but also a treasury for the considerable amount of Templar assets.

We will be discussing the role the Knights Templars played in the Reconquista and their activities in Europe later. Suffice it to say now that the Templars expanded their range of activities to include projects that went beyond their original goals.

The Templars built a web of stone castles and fortifications throughout Outremer. These bastions were practically invincible and could be easily defended. Moreover, they could receive reinforcements quickly. This military system gave a feeling of security within the Crusader States. It would be challenging for any opposing force to seize control of the area. Too much time and energy would be spent laying siege to these outposts, and the attacker could run out of money, troops, or both.

It would take considerable effort to conquer Outremer now that the Knights Templar had built castles. The only way to seize the Crusader States would be to have a larger and more disciplined army and a leader who was charismatic and a stellar warrior. It did not seem possible that these factors would all come together.

However, that is what happened in the late 12th century when all the pieces came together.

Chapter Five – Templars in Action: Prelude to a Crusade

"'Tell your people,' Salah al-Din told him, 'that we shall not treat them as your forebears treated us when they first took this city. As a child I was told of what Godfrey and Tancredo did to our people.'"

-Quote attributed to Saladin

The Second Crusade was a disaster, but the Knights Templar did not suffer much because of it. Indeed, the Templars' reputation was enhanced by their ability to behave as professional soldiers and protect the French Crusader contingent. The Templars were growing in notoriety and accumulated wealth.

You might say the Templar Order was the charity of choice in the Late Middle Ages. And the order received not only donations of money but also land grants and special privileges. The Templars were quickly becoming a state within those countries where they were active. They reported only to the pope, giving them considerable freedom.

The Crusader States benefited from the Muslim world's internal squabbling Muslim. Friction between the Shia and the Sunni factions of Islam occupied a lot of their time and allowed Outremer a period of peace, although it was a little unstable. There were still problems with brigands and occasional raids. Nevertheless, the Templars were able to manage things, and the construction of castles and other fortifications helped keep the peace.

Events became more challenging in the mid-11th century. The Fatimid Caliphate was starting to destabilize, and in 1171, the last of the caliphs died. The stage was set for one of the most extraordinary characters in the history of Islam.

His name was Salah al-Din Yusuf ibn Ayyub. He is popularly known in history as Saladin.

A Charismatic and Energetic Leader

Saladin was born around 1137 in Tikrit, which is located in what is now Iraq. His family was Kurdish, and his father and uncle were military leaders under Imad al-Din Zengi, the same man who conquered the County of Edessa. Saladin was destined for a life in the military and was part of a military expedition to Egypt that was commanded by his uncle in the service of Zengi's son, Nur al-Din.

Saladin was elevated to the position of vizier in Egypt after the death of his uncle in 1169. He became the governor of Egypt in 1171 when the last Fatimid caliph died. He was, at that time, governing in the name of Nur al-Din.

The Fatimids were a Shia dynasty, but Saladin was Sunni. He constantly talked about turning Egypt into a Sunni power base and was successful in doing that. When Nur al-Din died, Saladin returned to Syria and took control of the area, defeating Muslim rulers who controlled the major cities in the area. Ultimately, Saladin came into possession of Syria, Egypt, and Yemen. He had the Crusader States surrounded on three sides.

Plans for Outremer

Saladin wanted the Crusader States, pure and simple. There were some important reasons for wanting to take what did not belong to him. Outremer was a rich prize, and the trade and commerce would add significantly to Saladin's wealth. In addition, controlling the Levant would make troop movements from Egypt to the northern borders less complicated. Perhaps the most important reason for wanting the Crusader States was political.

Although Saladin had supplanted the Shia in Egypt, there were still dissidents who did not appreciate Sunni control. Saladin needed to instill loyalty and obedience, but he could not always do that by force of arms. But he could do it by enhancing his reputation in the Islamic world. Jerusalem was an essential part of the plan.

Jerusalem is the third holiest city of Islam. There were still hurt feelings about its loss and a desire to regain it. If Saladin were able to retake Jerusalem, his prestige in the Muslim world would skyrocket. It would be sufficient to keep potential rebels quiet in Egypt and elsewhere in his domain. By 1186, he had unified Syria, northern Mesopotamia, Egypt, and the areas of Palestine outside of the borders of the Crusader States. He needed an opportunity to launch a campaign against the Christians.[17]

Montgisard

Saladin's first opportunity arrived several years before, in 1177, with a failed Christian expedition. The king of Jerusalem, Baldwin IV, entered into an alliance with the Byzantine Empire to invade Egypt. That offensive did not happen, but Saladin raised an army to counter the invasion. He decided to take the initiative and, with an army of more than twenty-six thousand men, advanced into the Kingdom of Jerusalem.

Baldwin IV was only sixteen years old and suffering from leprosy (he is referred to as the Leper King in many historical accounts). Nevertheless, he rushed to Ascalon with a small force. Although Baldwin was able to take control of the city, he found himself besieged and surrounded by Saladin's army. Saladin was overconfident, and he took the bulk of his army up the coast for the sake of pillage and plunder.

Baldwin contacted the Templars, who were stationed at a fortress in Gaza. Baldwin received reinforcements from the Templars and issued a general call to arms to gather more troops. He caught up with Saladin and maneuvered the sultan into a battle at Montgisard. It was a victory for Baldwin. The support he received from the Templars made a significant difference. Saladin was able to retreat, but only a few of his soldiers survived. The final consequence of the battle happened in 1180 when Baldwin and Saladin established a two-year truce. It was a significant setback, but it was not the end of the sultan's ambitions.

Baldwin was victorious, but he was dying. Back then, leprosy was an incurable disease, and time was short for the king. He crowned his nephew, Baldwin V, in 1183, and the Leper King died two years later. A second truce for four years was negotiated with Saladin in 1185, but Baldwin V did not live to see the end of it. The Kingdom of Jerusalem

---

[17] History.com. (2021, August 5). *Saladin.* Retrieved from history.com: https://www.history.com/topics/africa/saladin.

was in a state of genuine confusion and was creating the situation for which Saladin was yearning.

Prelude to Disaster

Baldwin V's death began the cycle of events that ultimately permitted Saladin to achieve a significant personal goal. The Crusaders had no one to blame but themselves for what was going to happen. And the Knights Templar played a role in the calamity.

The successor to the young king was Guy de Lusignan, who was the brother-in-law of Baldwin IV. Unfortunately, he was not a very astute politician or diplomat and created unnecessary tension. One of Guy's supporters was a maverick named Raynald of Châtillon. He was the lord of Kerak, which was located southeast of the Dead Sea. This castle was close to the established caravan routes, and Raynald wanted to cause some trouble.

Ignoring the truce established in 1185, Raynald attempted a raid on Mecca. It was thwarted, and Raynald was lucky to escape alive. However, he did not learn his lesson from that bit of good fortune. He attacked a caravan that was passing near Kerak and refused to ransom the captives. Despite pressure from Guy, Raynald refused to relinquish his prisoners. That and the attempt to sack Mecca were all Saladin needed to end the truce. He called on all devout Muslims in the region to join him in an attack on the Kingdom of Jerusalem. It was going to be the united assault on the Crusader States the Christians had long dreaded.

A principal actor in the tragedy that followed was the Templar grand master, Gerard de Ridefort. Gerard was not a Templar when he first arrived in the Middle East. He was ultimately elected as grand master in 1184, and his election was not a good choice for the order. The man was clearly the wrong grand master at the wrong time.

De Ridefort was more of a hothead than a diplomat. When Saladin negotiated passage with the count of Tripoli to allow a Muslim army to enter Galilee, de Ridefort confronted Saladin in battle at the Spring of Cresson. It was a disaster for the Templars, and their grand master barely escaped with his life. Unfortunately for the Crusaders, he did.

Wiser minds cautioned Guy de Lusignan not to confront Saladin on the field of battle. There was a chance that diplomacy and negotiation could prevent severe consequences. Gerard de Ridefort can be credited with giving the king of Jerusalem terrible advice. Against the opinion of other, more sensible people, the Templar grand master advised the king of Jerusalem to move against Saladin. Guy de Lusignan took the advice and gathered an army that drew from the garrisons of all the cities and castles in the Crusader States. It included a large contingent of Templars.[18]

Horns of Hattin

It was all a major risk that Guy de Lusignan was willing to take. An outnumbered Crusader army advanced from Acre toward Lake Tiberias. The Templars were the primary troops protecting the rear and constantly fighting off Muslim attacks. They were moving across hot deserts while fighting Muslim skirmishers all along the way. The lack of water and intense heat exhausted the troops, and they still needed to come closer to Saladin's main army. Their progress was incredibly slow, and what little water they had was gradually consumed.

Their plight was made worse by the internal squabbling among the commanders, with one accusing the other of cowardice. Finally, the Crusaders camped on a ridge known as the Horns of Hattin.

Saladin was aware of the condition of the Christian soldiers and decided to make things even more challenging for them. As the Crusaders rested for the night, Saladin extended his lines to surround the Crusader camp and ordered his men to set fire to all the brush in the area. He waited until the hottest part of the day before he moved his troops, knowing that the Crusader army was suffering from thirst and would head in the direction of Lake Tiberias. And that is what happened. The Crusaders moved toward the lake and were blocked by the Muslim forces.

The ensuing battle was a massacre for the Crusaders. Overcome by heat and exhaustion, they fell before Saladin's troops. Their last stand failed, and the remaining Crusaders did nothing more than sit on the ground and wait to be taken as prisoners. Saladin's victory was total.

Saladin had a reputation for being a humane and chivalrous leader. That image was tarnished when he ordered the execution of all the surviving Templars and Knights Hospitaller. (Gerard de Ridefort was spared. Saladin saw to it that the captured Raynald of Châtillon was executed). The decision was more strategic than vengeance. Saladin

---

[18] Harper, I. G. (2023, February 12). *The Battle of the Horns of Hattin.* Retrieved from northumberlandkt.com: https://northumberlandkt.com/?page_id=3874.

knew the Templars were his primary opponents in the area. He respected their fighting prowess and was aware of what they could do in a fight.

Thus, he removed a significant obstacle to his plans by ordering their deaths. The Templars would not be there to resist his troops anymore. The way was open for the recapture of all of Outremer.

The Aftermath

The debacle at the Horns of Hattin affected Outremer. There were not enough troops to defend the Crusader States adequately, and the whole area was in jeopardy. Saladin's army moved almost unopposed and finally captured Jerusalem, making him the Islamic world's hero. Interestingly, Saladin did not attack the city. The defenders warned him that the Dome of the Rock would be destroyed if that happened. The surrender of Jerusalem was a peaceful transfer of power.[19]

Crusader cities and castles fell left and right until only Tyre was left as a Christian bastion in the Levant. Crusader resistance was now in complete shambles. Gerard de Ridefort was set free in the hopes that he would create some controversy within the remaining Crusader troops. He would eventually be killed, and his Templars could no longer offer any fight to the enemy. The entire situation was catastrophic for the Crusader States, which had routed Saladin only a few years before.

The demise of Outremer was avoidable. Saladin was an aggressive military commander, but he was also a pragmatist. He hated Raynald of Châtillon, but he had a great deal of respect for Raymond III, Count of Tripoli. If the king of Jerusalem had simply turned Raynald over to Saladin, that would have resolved many of the problems. The truce of 1185 might have been renewed, and if the new term were for ten years, it would have permitted the peace to outlive Saladin, who would die in 1193.

Instead, the incompetent management of the Crusader commanders led to grave consequences. A good portion of the blame can be attributed to Gerard de Ridefort. The Templar grand master did not understand diplomacy and negotiation. His input led to the defeat at the Horns of Hattin.

---

[19] Suhr, R. (2023, February 12). *Crusader Crucible: The Horns of Hattin.* Retrieved from warfarehistorynetwork.com: https://warfarehistorynetwork.com/crusader-crucible-the-horns-of-hattin/.

The result of all this was a complete triumph for the Muslims. Saladin had every reason to celebrate his victories. He achieved what he wanted: the end of the Crusader States. The Egyptian sultan was now the greatest force in the eastern Mediterranean, and there was no effective opposition to resist him. If Saladin had wanted to attack the Byzantine Empire, there would be no way to stop him effectively. He was at the height of his power, and there was nothing to prevent him from gaining even more prestige and territory.

However, he did not know that his circumstances were about to change and that he would soon be facing the greatest general of the Christian world.

Chapter Six – Templars in Action: The Third Crusade

"There was great sorrow among the Christians; many tears were shed on that day and all the men of the host were greatly troubled."

-William of Tyre's account of the reaction when Saladin did not deliver Christian prisoners as promised.

The news that Jerusalem had been taken stunned western Europe. The capture of the holy city by Saladin was disturbing enough, but the enormity of the overall catastrophe undoubtedly made the ruling class of the West nervous. Outremer was lost in only a few months. Tyre was the only city left of a sizable Christian presence in the Levant. Pilgrimages and trade were going to be affected by this, and even more importantly, trade relations that had developed over the last ninety years were in jeopardy.

Legend has it that Pope Urban III died of shock upon hearing the news of the Christian defeat at the Horns of Hattin. Whether that is true is a matter of conjecture and debate, but his successor, Pope Gregory VIII, seized the initiative and issued a papal bull. *Audita tremendi* raised the alarm and called for the Third Crusade. The stated reason was to take back Jerusalem and recover holy relics. Perhaps the more prominent reason for launching this campaign was to restore the Middle East to the status quo antebellum, which would be advantageous to Europe. Gregory's successor, Pope Clement III, took up the cause and preached vigorously for action.

The Third Crusade was going to be quite different from the Second Crusade. The papacy was able to get the commitment of three prominent European monarchs: Holy Roman Emperor Frederick Barbarossa, King Philip II of France, and King Richard I of England, who was known as Richard the Lionheart for his military prowess. This trio could command the public opinion and military power of Europe. What was contemplated was a mission that was on the scale of the First Crusade and would hopefully be as successful.

Richard and the Templars

The English Crown had a relationship of sorts with the Templars. As we mentioned earlier, Eleanor of Aquitaine, Richard's mother, had given the order special privileges in La Rochelle. Henry II, Richard's father, assessed the tax on every layperson in England and Wales to pay for the Third Crusade.[20]

It was known as the Saladin tithe, and Henry levied it in 1188 on his subjects. It is one of the first recorded taxes on personal income, and every layperson in the realm was taxed one-tenth of their personal income and movable property.

The tax was assessed by the dioceses and tax collectors, which included the local bishop, the dean of the local church, the local baron, and the Knights Templar. The only people exempt from the tithe were those who joined the Third Crusade.

Richard the Lionheart, who would take over as king shortly after the Third Crusade began, would have been familiar with the Knights Templar. He knew the value of the Templars as a fighting force. They were soldiers who were disciplined enough to avoid being easily routed in battle. So, Richard had the Knights Templars and its counterpart, the Knights Hospitaller, stationed at the vanguard (Templars) and the rearguard (Hospitallers) of the troop columns he commanded during the Third Crusade.[21]

Seizing Acre

Frederick Barbarossa drowned while on the way to Palestine. The Germans left the crusade, leaving the other two Crusader armies to do

---

[20] Tax Fitness.com. (2008, January 23). *1188-Saladin Tithe: One of the First Recorded Taxes on Income.* Retrieved from taxftness.com.au: https://taxfitness.com.au/Blog/1188-saladin-tithe.

[21] Walker, J. (2023, February 14). *Soldiers of God.* Retrieved from warfarehistorynetwork.com: https://warfarehistorynetwork.com/article/saldains-defeat-at-the-hands-of-the-knights-templar/

the fighting. Acre was under siege before the French and English contingents arrived. The French came to Acre first and were unable to break through the Muslim army defending the city. Richard and the English contingent arrived on June 8th, 1191. He had been delayed because he successfully captured Cyprus before setting out to the Holy Land.

Internal disputes between the French and the English caused some serious delays, but Richard's fleet was able to prevent any supplying to the Muslim garrison via the sea. So, the city was finally taken. The men guarding the garrison were granted their lives and could depart without their weapons once Saladin paid a hefty ransom, returned the fragments of the True Cross he had in his possession, and returned the 2,500 prisoners that were taken at Hattin. The men in the garrison were held as hostages until Saladin met the terms.

Medieval warfare was not a gentlemanly exercise; it could be extremely brutal and insensitive. Saladin had trouble raising the ransom and requested an extension. When the second extension expired, the sultan had yet to deliver the money, the True Cross, or the prisoners. Philip II had already left, so Richard was the only commander of the Crusader armies. Feeling insulted by Saladin's reluctance to comply with the terms, Richard took extreme action.

Richard's prerogative was how to deal with the Muslim hostages. He did not want his soldiers to think their king was weak, and he wanted Saladin to understand that he, Richard the Lionheart, was nobody to take lightly. He also could not afford to have 2,500 hostage troops kept prisoner in Acre while the Crusader army moved toward Jerusalem. So, Richard ordered the massacre of his hostages. All of them were killed.

Moving Down the Coast

Richard secured Acre and then started marching the Crusader army down the coast of the Levant. He was accompanied by the new grand master of the Templars, Robert de Sablé. De Sablé was a better-disciplined soldier and strategist than his predecessor, Gerard de Ridefort. He was not a Templar at the time of the other man's death but became one in order to be elected grand master. De Sablé was both a good general and a sharp negotiator. He was the grand master who purchased Cyprus from Richard.[22]

The Templars were now the owners of Cyprus, but they had difficulty holding onto it. The Cypriots did not appreciate the way they were treated and rose in rebellion. The small force of Templars sent to govern the island quickly returned to Acre. De Sablé returned Cyprus to Richard, who then sold it to Guy de Lusignan, the king of Jerusalem. The purchase and the return of Cyprus were perhaps embarrassing, but the transactions did not harm the Templars. On the contrary, they were now part of a crusading army that was showing signs of great success, as cities and fortresses down the coast surrendered to Richard.

Saladin did not desert Palestine but recognized that he was up against a sizable opponent. The Crusaders under Richard marched in a disciplined formation, and it became abundantly clear Richard would not engage in a battle where he would be at a disadvantage. So, Saladin had to wait for his opportunity while harassing the Crusaders as they moved south.

Muslim efforts to draw the Crusaders into a military disaster were not working. Why weren't Saladin's tactics successful the way they had been before? The answer is simple. The Crusaders were now following the example of the Templars and the Hospitallers. The discipline and restraint these two orders exhibited and enforced kept the troops in line. Richard was also listening to the advice of both military orders. The English king understood that the Templars and Hospitallers were familiar with Saladin and how the Muslim commander operated. The Crusaders had been fooled in the past. However, they were no longer duped by Saladin's disruptive efforts thanks to the Templars and Hospitallers. The columns held orderly rank and file as they marched.

Battle of Arsuf

Richard moved his army south to take the port of Jaffa. Once the city was seized, the intention was to move the troops inland to take Jerusalem. The English king hugged the coast so that the soldiers might quickly be supplied by his fleet. Richard wanted to avoid another crisis like Hattin. The Crusader army moved early in the morning to avoid the intense heat of the day, and the leaders chose campsites that had access to a water supply.

---

[22] erenow.net. (2023, February 14). *Grand Masters 1191-1292/9.* Retrieved from erenow.net: https://erenow.net/postclassical/the-real-history-behind-the-templars/23.php

Saladin shadowed the Crusader army, hoping to find a situation where he could break its ranks. He harassed the flanks of the Crusaders, hoping that there might be a chance where his cavalry could sweep in. The defensive formations of the Crusaders benefited them. They successfully fought off three major attacks as the columns continued their progress.

Saladin finally decided to make a stand and chose Arsuf as the place where he would finally confront Richard in a major battle. He intended to initiate combat with a succession of attacks and feigned retreats. Saladin's troops began to attack the morning of September 7th, 1191.

The Crusaders were hit with hit-and-run tactics as planned. The Crusaders sustained losses from these maneuvers, but they did not break rank. Saladin began to concentrate on the rearguard, which was a clever move. He hoped increased assaults on the rear would force the rest of the Crusader army to turn around and go to its rescue, which could cause confusion and allow the Muslim army to launch a successful offensive. Saladin centered his attack on that part of the Crusader column, which was where the Knights Hospitaller was concentrated.

Formally known as the Order of Knights of the Hospital of Saint John of Jerusalem, the Hospitallers were another military order, although their original purpose was to support the hospital and care for the sick. However, they gradually turned into a defense force to protect the Holy Land. They were as tough in battle as their Templar counterparts.

Richard gave strict orders not to counterattack any Muslim assault. He hoped to wait until there was sufficient evidence that Saladin's troops were getting tired. Nevertheless, the rearguard action faced earnest assaults from the Muslim forces. Garnier de Nablus, the commander of the Hospitallers, finally ignored the command and ordered a charge. They were able to break through the ranks of the enemy.

Richard was not happy with this development, but he realized the Hospitallers needed to be reinforced. So, he ordered the Templars to attack Saladin's left flank. Richard then personally led the attack against the Muslim center. It shattered the enemy's formations and forced Saladin to retreat.

The victory at Arsuf was important because it avenged the loss at Hattin and boosted the morale of the Crusaders. They continued their march and eventually captured Jaffa.[23]

Jaffa and Beyond

Richard established his new headquarters at Jaffa and sent peace feelers to Saladin, hoping that negotiations would produce some solid results. But unfortunately, the initial effort failed, and the Crusaders marched to Ascalon, where they rebuilt demolished fortifications.

Harsh weather compelled Richard to call off an assault on Jerusalem, and he remained in Ascalon for the winter months. The Templars eventually moved into Ramleh, and their foraging expedition secured over two hundred oxen. Finally, the order set up winter headquarters in Gaza.

The Third Crusade was a military success by this point. Arsuf was a significant setback for Saladin. He was still able to harass the Crusaders, but his army was not strong enough to launch a powerful attack. The beginning of 1192 looked promising, but non-military matters were starting to disrupt the Crusaders' plans.

Conrad, Marquis of Montferrat, was a claimant to the crown of Jerusalem. He was secretly negotiating with Saladin to attack the Crusaders and cede several maritime cities to Saladin in return for the sultan's support of his claim to Jerusalem. However, Conrad was assassinated before the deal was finalized. The question of who was to rule Jerusalem involved the Templars, who persuaded Guy de Lusignan to abdicate in favor of Henry, Count of Champagne. However, there was still more trouble brewing in the Christian camp.

Richard received news from England that his brother, John, whom Richard had left in charge of things, was plotting against him. An even more severe threat was coming from his former Crusader comrade in arms, Philip II. The French king was stirring up trouble, and Richard was being placed in jeopardy. The English king realized he had to return home as soon as possible. There are only two alternatives for Richard: the successful capture of Jerusalem, which would end the crusade, or negotiations with Saladin.

Richard began an advance on Jerusalem on June 11th, 1192. Saladin took advantage of this by attacking Jaffa. Richard was able to regain Jaffa with an amphibious assault, but it was becoming clear that taking

---

[23] ThoughtCo.com. (2023, February 15). *The Battle of Arsuf in the Crusades.* Retrieved from thoughtco.com: https://www.thoughtco.com/the-crusades-battle-of-arsuf-2360710.

Jerusalem by force was a bridge too far. The Templars and Hospitallers recognized the futility of trying to take the holy city. They advised Richard not to attempt a siege of Jerusalem, claiming there was no chance of success. Richard concluded that the military seizure of Jerusalem was no longer feasible. The way was open to a negotiated settlement.

A final settlement was reached that allowed Christian pilgrims to visit Jerusalem and the Holy Sepulchre. In addition, the cities of Tyre, Jaffa, and Acre were to remain in the hands of the Crusaders, but the fortifications erected at Ascalon were to be destroyed. A three-year truce was negotiated.

Richard was now free to leave the Holy Land, and he did not waste any time. The English fleet returned to England by way of the Strait of Gibraltar, but Richard went in a different direction. The Templars furnished Richard with one of the Templar ships and four knights as bodyguards. Disguising himself as a Knight Templar, Richard and his attendants set sail for an Adriatic port. The Third Crusade was officially over.[24]

The Final Analysis

Historians routinely dismiss the Third Crusade as a failed effort. They note that Richard the Lionheart came close to Jerusalem but could not take it. The English king had to settle for a negotiated compromise. We submit that this enterprise was a draw: both sides gained a little and lost a little.

Saladin still had control of Jerusalem and had the prestige of being the conqueror of Islam's third holiest city. Nevertheless, he did not succeed in destroying the Latin East. The negotiated settlement permitted Acre to remain in Christian hands. Christian pilgrimage rights were guaranteed, and a three-year truce was put into effect. Although the Christian presence in the Middle East was significantly reduced, it would still be there. Saladin did achieve most of his original goal, only to see those gains gradually evaporate in a few years like April snow.

Richard the Lionheart was frustrated in his effort to retake Jerusalem, but he still gained something. Acre was a formidable city and could be

---

[24] Esq., C. A. (2023, February 15). *The Knights Templars.* Retrieved from hellenicaworld.com: https://www.hellenicaworld.com/History/CGAddison/en/TheKnightsTemplars.html#CHAPTER_V.

used as a staging point for further action against Muslims in the area. Even better, Richard had taken Cyprus. This island was like a dagger pointed at the throat of any Muslim ruler in the Levant. It could be used as a supply depot and furnish future Christian armies with the manpower and food required to conduct a later campaign in the area. Cyprus and Acre had the potential of making a later effort more successful. Saladin died in 1193, and his death impacted the balance of power in the Muslim world. The Crusaders finally had some breathing room.

It should be noted that the Crusaders did take back sizable pieces of territory that Saladin had seized only a few years before. The gloom and doom scenario confronting the Latin East in 1187 had subsided by 1193. However, it would require delicate diplomacy and negotiation for the Crusader States to survive. Thus, they needed to rely on more than the force of arms because their enemy was larger and better organized.

The Knights Templar made off rather nicely in this enterprise. Richard sold Cyprus to the order, which held the island for several months before giving it back to Richard. Ultimately, it was given to Guy de Lusignan to compensate for his previous abdication.

Meanwhile, Templars kept their castles in Cyprus and used the island for military purposes in the years to come. There are still remnants of Templar fortifications on the island. Additionally, the order still had its reputation intact, despite any setbacks encountered during the Third Crusade. It could be argued that this was the high point in the history of the Knights Templar. They were a force to be reckoned with.

Their power and influence would be sorely tested in the years to come. Outremer still existed, but power politics and military setbacks were going to take a toll on the Knights Templar.

Chapter Seven – Templars in Action: The Later Crusades

"How shall I begin to tell of the deeds wrought by these nefarious men! Alas, the images, which ought to have been adored, were trodden underfoot! Alas, the relics of the holy martyrs were thrown into unclean places!"

-Niketas Choniates describing the sack of Constantinople

The Treaty of Jaffa was signed on September 1st, 1192, between Saladin and Richard the Lionheart. The three-year truce assured that Outremer would be quiet for a while. This, of course, did not mean political hibernation or a guarantee of peace. Events were happening that would shape the fate of the region.

Grand Master Robert De Sablé was killed in 1193. He was killed in action supposedly by a member of the Assassins, a covert Muslim order. Gilbert Horal succeeded him. Saladin died seven months after the signing of the Treaty of Jaffa. The one man who could unite Islam in a fight against the Crusaders left behind family members and followers who all fought for pieces of his empire. This state of confusion benefited the Christians.

The Islamic coalition Saladin created dissolved, and the various Muslim states went back to their internecine warfare and squabbling. The Crusader States would not have to worry about a major army threatening them and could enjoy the benefits of peace, no matter how shaky it might be at times.

The consequences of the Third Crusade could have been better for Europe. Richard came very close to taking Jerusalem completely. But Outremer had nearly been conquered by Saladin, and his attempt to get rid of the Crusader States was not successful. Major ports in the Levant were again in Christian hands, and the pilgrimage trade, which had been interrupted by hostilities, was now back in action, and the three-year truce would allow tourists and money to flow freely into the area. The Templars and the Hospitallers commanded the internal defenses, and commercial enterprises had a new lease on life. Western Europe was able to get an excellent deal and did its very best to trainwreck it.

The Fourth Crusade

The primary reason for the Fourth Crusade was that Jerusalem was in the hands of the infidels. So what? The Christians must have forgotten that Muslims had control of Jerusalem for four centuries before the First Crusade. There was not much of a problem during the years following the Third Crusade because the pilgrims had access to the holy shrines. The Treaty of Jaffa affirmed those rights. The original truce might have been extended and included other benefits for pilgrims and the Crusader States, so taking Jerusalem was not a necessity. However, there may have been ulterior motives covered by a smokescreen of another crusade.

There was a religious division in the Christian world that was just as troublesome as what existed between Shia and Sunni Muslims. The Great Schism of 1054 created a rift between the Roman Catholic Church and the Eastern Orthodox Church. The Byzantine Empire considered itself the greatest defender of Christendom, which it had been for several centuries. Western Europe fought to regain parts of Italy from Byzantium in the past, and there were disputes as the years passed. There was some recent Western resentment of the Byzantines based on a claim that Constantinople had not done enough in the Third Crusade. For their part, Byzantines considered Western Crusaders more opportunistic than religious. The animosities were there, and the Fourth Crusade would bring them boiling to the surface.

A Call to Arms

Saladin was barely cold in his grave when Pope Innocent III, the newly elected pontiff, called for the Fourth Crusade in August 1198. The Crusaders were given the standard recruitment incentive of remission of all sins, but Pope Innocent would sweeten the deal. The same remission of sins would be awarded to anyone who paid for a replacement soldier to fight in their stead. That extra benefit was intended to assure that there would be sufficient money to conduct a successful crusade.

The pope's timing was terrible. Disputes between the major powers of western Europe meant powerful rulers were too busy to give a lot of support. Richard the Lionheart, the Third Crusade's hero, had been killed in 1199 while besieging a castle in France. There was going to be no celebrity leader. Instead, Boniface I, Marquis of Montferrat, was chosen as the overall commander. There was trouble enough, and having the second-tier Western nobility in charge of the Fourth Crusade was not the solution. However, things would get worse before anything got better.[25]

A Confusion of Objectives

The Crusaders planned to take a different route to Jerusalem. Instead of landing troops on the coast of Palestine, the Fourth Crusade would attack Egypt. The rationale was that Egypt was the power center of the Middle East, and by winning the ancient land of the pharaohs, negotiations might permit the return of Jerusalem to Christian hands. However, invading Egypt required a large amphibious assault and an enormous navy.

Ships were available in Venice. The Venetians had become an essential player in the eastern Mediterranean and were commercial rivals of Constantinople. Venice agreed to supply the ships but at a price. The Crusaders needed to come up with the money to pay for the use of the Venetian fleet, and their enormous debt would influence future events.

Venice was required to have ships available to send over thirty thousand Crusaders to Egypt. But unfortunately, there was little interest in Europe to conduct another crusade less than ten years after the last one ended.

Around twelve thousand Crusaders were available for the new crusade. The force was insufficient for a successful Egyptian campaign. Nevertheless, the Venetians wanted their money for the ships they had provided. To pay off their enormous IOU, the Crusaders attacked the Adriatic seaport of Zara and pillaged it. The assault infuriated the pope, but what the Crusaders did next was even more horrifying.

---

[25] Cartwright, M. (2018, September 3). *Fourth Crusade*. Retrieved from worldhistory.org: https://www.worldhistory.org/Fourth_Crusade/.

Constantinople was the capital of the Byzantine Empire and the central hub of commerce in the eastern Mediterranean. An incredible amount of trade went through the Bosporus, and the Venetians wanted to eliminate this competitor. The crusading army was still in debt to the Venetians and sailed to Constantinople, whose former co-emperor, Alexios IV Angelos, requested their help in getting the throne back. The Crusaders did, but Alexios was unable to pay them the sum he had promised. When he was murdered, the Crusaders realized they would never be paid back and decided to plunder Constantinople.[26]

It was a classic example of cutting one's nose off to spite one's face. Constantinople and the Byzantine Empire had been a primary defense against Muslim incursions into Europe. They had held off Islamic forces for centuries only to be knifed in the back by those whom the Byzantines ought to have been able to trust. The Crusaders set up a Latin Kingdom on the city's rubble, but that did not change the results of the Fourth Crusade. Byzantium was irrevocably weakened, and the Fourth Crusade was the beginning of the collapse of a thousand-year-old empire. The Fourth Crusade also solidified the divide between Eastern and Western Christianity.

The Great Schism between the Roman Catholic Church and the Eastern Orthodox Church occurred in 1054. Tensions between those two branches of Christianity could be as volatile as the fights between Shia and Sunni Muslims. Now, the separation between the two branches of Christianity was permanent. Christianity was no longer a unified front against invading forces.

What were the Templars doing while all this mayhem and plunder was going on? It appears the Templars were on the sidelines during the Fourth Crusade. Individual brothers may have followed the Crusaders, but other than helping raise money for the effort, the order was not formally involved as a fighting unit.

This did not mean they did not benefit from what happened. What is interesting is that after the Fourth Crusade, the Templars received property in Greece. The Templars did not partake in the fighting, but they did get rewards from the fall of Constantinople.[27]

---

[26] History Crunch.com. (2023, February 18). *Fourth Crusade.* Retrieved from historycrunch.com: https://www.historycrunch.com/fourth-crusade.html#/.

[27] Nicholson, H. J. (2003, May 1). *The Motivations of the Templars in Their Involvement in the*

The Fifth Crusade

Pope Innocent did not give up on his desire to take Jerusalem, despite the unexpected failure and embarrassment of the Fourth Crusade. He started to organize the Fifth Crusade almost immediately after the end of the Fourth. The strategy that the pontiff had in mind seems odd, but it did have some logic to it.

Egypt was ruled by the Ayyubid dynasty, which Saladin had established. If the Crusaders attempted to take Jerusalem by landing in Palestine, they could expect to be vigorously attacked from the south by the Egyptians. Instead of waiting for that assault, the new crusade would steal a march on its enemy and attack Egypt. If successful, the crusade could negotiate a return of Jerusalem to the control of the Western Christians. The strategy was risky, but Innocent thought it was a gamble worth taking.

There was a truce in existence between the Crusader States and the Ayyubids that was supposed to last until the end of 1217. Innocent issued the papal bull *Quia maior* in 1213, which called for a new crusade. A conciliar decree, *Ad liberandam*, was published in 1215 to do the planning. There was sufficient time until the end of the 1217 truce to prepare for a successful enterprise.

The Fifth Crusade was an all-hands-on-deck affair. Innocent was able to secure the support of the king of Hungary, the duke of Austria, and the king of Jerusalem. Furthermore, the Templars, the Hospitallers, and a new order, the Teutonic Knights, were included. The Templars were responsible for collecting donations, and this effort appeared to have an excellent chance of succeeding. However, there was one big problem.

Innocent died and was succeeded by Honorius III. Innocent wanted the church to lead the crusade so as to avoid the mistakes that happened in the last effort. Honorius followed through with this and appointed Pelagius of Albano to lead it. That was a mistake, as Pelagius had no military experience. As a result, the Fifth Crusade was shot in the foot before the ships carrying the troops left port.

Fourth Crusade and Its Aftermath. Retrieved from researchgate.net: https://www.researchgate.net/publication/264646303_The_Motivations_of_the_Hospitallers_and_Templars_in_their_involvement_in_the_Fourth_Crusade_and_its_aftermath.

Siege of Damietta

Damietta is a port city at the mouth of the Nile where it flows into the Mediterranean Sea. The consensus of the Fifth Crusade leaders was that control of this port would also mean control of the Nile. It would be the base from which they could conquer Egypt and, in turn, recapture Jerusalem. Crusader ships arrived at Acre in March 1218. Those ships assigned to take Damietta set sail in late May from Acre. On board the vessels were groups of Templars.

The Crusaders arrived on the Egyptian coastline on May 27th, 1218, and established a beachhead on May 29th. They faced a city with three walls, twenty towers, and a moat. The most impressive defensive structure was the river tower, which protected the city's fortress and was also an anchoring point for a chain that stretched across the harbor.

That river tower was the Crusaders' primary objective. They were unsuccessful until one of the Crusader preachers, Oliver of Paderborn, designed a floating siege tower wrapped in Greek-fire-resistant animal skins. The floating siege tower allowed the Crusaders to use their siege weapons, and the tower eventually fell on August 24th, 1218. A significant loss to the Templars occurred not long afterward. The fourteenth grand master, William of Chartres, died.

The siege of Damietta continued to grind on. The Templars were in the thick of the action along with the other military orders, but the defensive walls of the city continued to hold firm. Finally, in September 1219, Damietta fell to the Crusaders. It was at this point that Sultan al-Kamil of Egypt made an astounding offer. He was willing to give Jerusalem back to the Crusaders with a thirty-year truce included. All he wanted was for the Crusaders to leave Egypt. In other words, he was offering to give the Crusaders what they wanted most of all. Some Crusader leaders wanted to take the sultan up on this offer, but others, including the Templars and the Hospitallers, wanted to reject the offer.

It may sound incredible that the Crusaders turned down the offer of Jerusalem, but there were a few reasons for it. The Transjordan fortresses controlled by the Ayyubids were not part of the deal, and without those, Jerusalem could easily be retaken. Additionally, there were serious doubts as to whether the truce would be honored. Finally, the Muslims could renege on everything once the Crusaders returned to

Europe.[28]

The crusade continued and eventually turned in favor of the Egyptians. Al-Kamil ordered the sluice gates of the Nile to be opened so that the ground was flooded under the feet of the Crusaders. The sultan then offered new terms that included the return of Damietta, the freedom of all enslaved Muslims in Acre and Tyre, and an eight-year truce. The Crusaders were expected to leave Egypt. Faced with possible starvation, the Christian leaders agreed and left.

The Templars showed themselves to be dependable fighters, but something else came out of the Fifth Crusade that benefited the order. The Templars not only collected donations for this crusade, but they also accounted for the money that was collected. The Knights Templar was handling financial transfers and moving money around. The Templars' work was so impressive that the pope used no other financial intermediaries. In other words, the papacy trusted the Templars with enormous sums of money.

The Sixth Crusade

Frederick II was an amazing man for his time. He was a Renaissance man centuries before that term came into use, but he was referred to as *stupor mundi* ("wonder of the world"). He was the Holy Roman emperor and ruler of Sicily as well. Frederick was brilliant, and he was able to accomplish what Richard the Lionheart could not do.

Frederick was not involved in the Fifth Crusade and wanted to make up for his absence. He proposed another crusading effort, which the Holy Roman Empire would bankroll. Frederick and his army faced an immediate problem once they reached Outremer: their force was smaller than the army raised for the Fifth Crusade, and they were facing a significantly larger opposing force. Frederick opted for a tactic that was rarely used in earlier crusading efforts. He tried negotiation.

Al-Kamil was still the sultan of Egypt. Frederick contacted him and pretended that the crusading army was much larger than it really was. He approached al-Kamil at the right time. The Egyptian ruler was fighting a rebellion in Syria, and he did not need a distraction. Frederick proposed a ten-year truce in exchange for Jerusalem, Nazareth, and a few other small towns. The sultan agreed, and on March 17th, 1229, Frederick II

[28] Prester John. (2021, September 4). *Prester John 3: The Fifth Crusade.* Retrieved from humancircuspodcast.com:.

entered Jerusalem.[29]

Europe was overjoyed at the news, but the Templars were not as enthusiastic. The Sixth Crusade was the first time that the Catholic Church was not fully involved in the endeavor. Additionally, Frederick had been excommunicated, and the Templars were not thrilled to be dealing with a man who was an apostate. The terms of the agreement with al-Kamil stipulated that the Temple Mount was to remain in the hands of the Muslims. Suffice it to say that the Templars and the Holy Roman emperor did not get along, but Frederick had achieved a triumph through diplomacy that a force of arms was not able to deliver.

The Later Crusades

The Middle East was rarely peaceful for any length of time. As-Salih Ayyub was the sultan of Egypt when new animosities developed. There was not much left of the crusading spirit, but it was still present in the French king, Louis IX.

The French took up where the Fifth Crusade left off. Damietta was once again attacked and seized. This crusade saw the Ayyubids toppled from the throne to be replaced by the Mamluks. The new rulers were a force to be reckoned with. The Mamluks were professional soldiers; they were even able to defeat the Mongols at one point. The new Egyptian regime was more than a match for the Knights Templar.

The Seventh Crusade ended with Louis IX's capture, and the city of Jerusalem was once again taken by the Muslims. The Eighth Crusade, whose goal was to take Tunis, ended in disappointment, and that was the final effort by western Europe to take control of the Holy Land.

The years between the Fifth Crusade and the Eighth Crusade witnessed a decline in the prowess of the Knights Templar as a fighting force in Outremer. The Templars were no longer the overbearing presence on the battlefield they once were, and they suffered a series of defeats. However, this did not mean the Templars were finished. On the contrary, while there was a great deal of frustration in the East, the Templars would prove to be highly successful against the Muslims in battles waged at the western end of the Mediterranean.

---

[29] History Learning.com. (2015, January 1). *The Sixth Crusade.* Retrieved from historylearning.com: https://historylearning.com/medieval-england/the-crusades/sixth-crusade/.

Chapter Eight – Reconquista

"In mea marchia contra Sarracenos." ("In my march against the Muslims.")

-Ramon Berenguer III giving Granyena to the Knights Templar

The Muslims invaded the Iberian Peninsula in the 8th century and successfully overthrew the Visigoth dynasty. They conquered most of Spain and Portugal and ruled them for centuries. Islamic Spain is often portrayed as a place of learning and culture, with architecture such as the Alhambra and the intellectual stimulation of Córdoba coming down to us through the centuries. It appears to have been an enlightened, benevolent place. Yet the Christians wanted it back and wanted the Muslims out.

Why was that? After all, our image of Al-Andalus (the Iberian Peninsula) has been one of tolerance and intelligence. What would make anybody want to expel the Muslims?

Sometimes, we must strip off the veneer to look at history's hard surface and rough texture. There were times when Spain was enjoying a golden age, and there were also periods when repression was taking center stage. Christians and Jews were second-class citizens and forced to pay a tax called the jizya. The testimony of a Christian against a Muslim was not admissible in court. A Christian could not have Muslim servants. A Christian who killed a Muslim was inevitably condemned to death, even if the Christian was only defending himself. The Almohad Caliphate practiced forced conversion of both Christians and Jews. The repression was so intense that the Christian community in Al-Andalus was practically gone by the 12th century.[30]

An atrocity that stands out in the history of Islamic Spain is the Granada massacre of 1066. On December 30th, 1066, approximately four thousand Jews were killed by an Arab mob in Granada. Episodes such as this were sufficient to convince the non-Muslim population that a regime change in the Iberian Peninsula was necessary for them to survive. As a result, the Reconquista had an enthusiastic following.[31]

It is essential to remember that the Reconquista involved two areas within the Iberian Peninsula: Spain and Portugal. The Knights Templar were involved in both regions and contributed significantly to the advancement of the Christian cause. We are going to refer to Muslims as Moors in this chapter for the sake of clarity, as that was the common name given to the followers of Islam in Iberia at the time.

The Reconquista

Enter the Knights Templar

The original caliphate of Al-Andalus was gone by the 11th century. In its place were the taifas, which were individual Moorish principalities that identified with distinct Islamic ethnic groups. For example, the Berbers were predominant on the southern coast. These little kingdoms fought amongst themselves, so there was an opportunity for the Christian kingdoms in the north to exploit the divisions. Those Spanish kingdoms were León, Castile, and Aragon. Each of these kingdoms wanted to expand the Christian presence in Spain, which made participation in their wars against the Moors attractive, but each had its own political objectives as well.

The Spanish kingdoms were encouraged not to be involved in the First Crusade since they had a significant battle to wage against Islam in the Iberian Peninsula. After the First Crusade, the Iberian Peninsula was recognized as a crusade. Pope Paschal II further legitimized that struggle by granting the remission of sins to anyone involved in driving the Moors

---

[30] Imatz, A. (2020, September 1). *Al-Andalus: A History Contaminated by Political Correctness.* Retrieved from thepostil.com: https://www.thepostil.com/al-andalus-a-history-contaminated-by-political-correctness/.

[31] Welton, B. (2016, August 16). *10 Overlooked Facts About the Spanish Reconquest.* Retrieved from listverse.com: https://listverse.com/2016/08/16/10-overlooked-facts-about-the-spanish-reconquest/.

from Spain. The Knights Templar were committed to their objectives in Outremer and were hesitant to be involved militarily elsewhere. That attitude soon changed.

Ramon IV of Barcelona was made an honorary Templar in 1134 and became a very generous benefactor of the order. He joined the County of Barcelona to the Kingdom of Aragon in 1143 and vigorously persuaded the Templars to participate in wars against the Moors.

The fight was a series of wars that were conquests, as the name "Reconquista" implies. It may appear a bit far-fetched, but a rationale for fighting in Spain developed that argued by defeating the Moors there, the road to Jerusalem could be opened through North Africa. Apparently, it did not matter that this didn't make much sense. Spain is thousands of miles away from the Middle East, but it was still a justification for the Templars to participate in the Spanish wars.

The Moors provided a greater justification for fighting in Spain. The Almohads were a fundamentalist Islamic sect that came from North Africa. They seized control of Moorish-held Spain in the early 12th century and were actively forcing conversions on Christians. This intolerance gave sufficient impetus for the Templars to become more actively involved in Spain.[32]

The New Crusade

A new crusade was called for in 1212 with the backing of the pope. This was an endeavor that included the major Spanish Christian kingdoms of Aragon, Castile, and Navarre. They combined forces to end the Moorish occupation of the lower part of Spain. Included in the ranks of the Christian troops were the Spanish knights of the Order of Santiago and the Order of Calatrava. The Knights Templar were also part of the fighting force.

The Christians face d an extreme challenge. The Almohad caliphs were in control of mountain passes in the Sierra Morena and had sufficient troops to fight against any invasion of their lands. The chances of a Christian victory were small.[33]

---

[32] Bevan, R. (2023, February 20). *The Templars in Iberia: The Reconquista and the Spanish Crusades.* Retrieved from history.co.uk: https://www.history.co.uk/shows/lost-relics-of-the-knights-templar/articles/the-templars-in-iberia-the-reconquista-and-the.

[33] Turney, S. (2020, July 25). *The Templars and the Reconquest of Spain.* Retrieved from historiamag.com: https://www.historiamag.com/templars-and-the-reconquest-of-spain/.

Las Navas de Tolosa

We have to take any declaration that a specific battle turned the course of history with a grain of salt. However, there are a few, and one of them was fought on July 16th, 1212. This battle is credited with changing the course of history in Spain and significantly adding to the success of the Reconquista.

Christian troops reached the foothills of the Sierra Morena range in July. The terrain hampered them, and they didn't quite know how to cross the mountains into Moorish territory. The Almohads appeared to have tight control of all the mountain passes. At least, they thought they did.

A legend of the battle is that a local shepherd knew of a gorge that was unknown to the Moors. This sheepherder, Martin Halaja, supposedly led the Christian forces through the canyon, and they crept past the Moorish fortifications. The Christians then faced a surprised enemy at Las Navas de Tolosa on July 16th. The result of the battle was a significant victory for the Christians. But more importantly, the Spanish now had a pass through the Sierra Morena and access to the Moorish south.[34]

The Knights Templar fought in the rearguard of the Christian army. After the battle, the king of Castile bragged that the Christian casualties were insignificant. That is not true. The Templars sustained very heavy losses. Among the Templar dead was the Portuguese grand master. Nevertheless, Las Navas de Tolosa was a significant victory and significantly boosted the morale of the Christian soldiers.[35]

The victory at Las Navas de Tolosa caused a domino effect in Spain. The Christians now had access to the south, particularly Guadalquivir Valley. Christian military forces poured directly into the exposed area. Córdoba fell to the Castilians in June 1236 after a short siege. The great Mosque of Córdoba, a gem of Moorish architecture, was officially cleansed, and Mass was said within its walls. Valencia capitulated to Aragon in 1238, and Castile took Murcia in 1243. Seville once again became a Christian city in 1248. With the fall of Seville, the only Moorish outpost in Spain was the Kingdom of Granada, which would fall

[34] Watson, C. C. (2023, February 20). *The Battle of Las Navas de Tolosa.* Retrieved from andalucia.com: https://www.andalucia.com/spainsmoorishhistory/las-navas-de-tolosa.htm.
[35] Jones, D. (2017). *The Templars: The Rise and Spectacular Fall of God's Holy Warriors.* New York, New York: Penguin Books.

in the 15th century.

The Knights Templar had a hand in all of this, but their greatest success was not on the battlefield. The Spanish kings rewarded the order for all it did to advance the Christian cause. Large tracts of land and other endowments were bestowed on the Templars in gratitude for their service. These lands and donations would become a significant part of their financial position.

Templar castles in Spain acted as defenses of the Christian territories. Some were built by the order, but others were Moorish fortresses renovated by the Templars. Several of these castles are still standing today and commemorate the effort and sacrifice of the Knights Templar.

The Portuguese Reconquista

The Reconquista in Portugal has been slightly overshadowed by what happened in Spain, partly due to the size of the territory. Portugal is much smaller and clings to the Atlantic coast. Nevertheless, there was a struggle in Portugal that resulted in power shifting away from the Moors to the Christians in the 13th century. The Battle of Las Navas de Tolosa saw the Portuguese involved in the triumph over the Moors. The last Moorish stronghold in Portugal, the region of Algarve, fell to the Christians when Faro was captured in 1249.

The Templars had been in Portugal for a century before this victory. They were present at Santarém when it was taken by Afonso Henriques, who rewarded the order with land and property. The Templars also participated in the final capture of Lisbon.

A significant contribution of the Templars to the Portuguese struggle came with the siege of Alcácer do Sal. The city was a frontier outpost of the Almohads. The Moors used it as a base for raids into Portugal, and enslaved people were exported from Alcácer to Morocco. The decision was made to get rid of this thorn in the side of the Portuguese. The siege began on July 30th, 1217, and Spanish Grand Master Pedro Alvarez Alvito led the Templars. The city finally fell on October 18th, 1217.

The Castles and Property of the Templars in Iberia

The Christian monarchs of Iberia appreciated the services of the Templars and were generous in their rewards to the order. The rewards included numerous castles and other properties in Portugal and Spain, giving evidence of the prominence of the Templars in these regions.

However, these were not just shows of gratitude. Such gifts had a very practical side. There was always the chance the Moors would return, and the Kingdom of Granada was a possible staging point for any reinvasion of the Iberian Peninsula. Whatever the Templars received came with the understanding that the Christian monarchs would be able to call on the services of the order if needed.

Northern Spain has a significant religious route going through it, the Camino De Santiago. This is a pilgrimage path to the shrine of Santiago de Compostela. In the Middle Ages, Santiago de Compostela was as famous as Canterbury for the religious faithful. There are several routes along the Camino to Santiago, and the French Way is one of them. The Castle of Ponferrada was intended to protect the French Way.

The Templars took control of the castle in 1178 and turned it into a prominent defensive position. Three defensive belts were built on eight thousand square meters of surface, making it a dominant presence in the northern region of Spain.

The Templars were routinely given fortresses that once belonged to the Moors. The Castle of Montalban defended the Torcon River and was a significant defensive position until the Battle of Las Navas de Tolosa. The Templars also had command of Jerez de los Caballeros, which was situated in a dangerous border zone.[36]

Portugal has the honor of having the most important collection of Templar castles outside of the Middle East. These fortifications served their purpose during the Reconquista as defensive positions and were also essential administrative locations for the Templar Order.

The Castle of Almourol is situated on an island on the River Tagus. It was originally a Moorish fortress, and the Templars rebuilt it into a significant military bastion. Tomar was the headquarters of the Knights Templar in Portugal. Its importance grew as the Templars became a more significant financial powerhouse in Europe.[37]

It is understandable that some of these castles became less defensive structures and more administrative. This is because the power of the

[36] Fascinating Spain. (2023, February 21). *Impressive Templar Castles in Spain.* Retrieved from fascinatingspain.com: https://fascinatingspain.com/place-to-visit/the-best-of/impressive-templar-castles-in-spain/ .

[37] Stables, D. (2021, October 3). *On the Trail of the Knights Templar in Portugal.* Retrieved from roughguides.com.

Moors was broken in the 13th century. They were no longer the threat they once posed to Christians in the peninsula, and the Templar castles became less strategic militarily. However, it did not mean that these buildings were abandoned.

Over time, the Templars developed into a significant financial force in Europe, with holdings and properties spread all over the continent. These lands needed to be managed and administrated effectively. Using the castles for more administrative purposes and securing the necessary money to conduct more crusades made sense.

The Templars were part of the Christian success story of the Reconquista. Their contributions in the battles, such as Las Navas de Tolosa, were significant, and their command of fortifications ensured that the Moors would not regain what they lost. The Iberian Peninsula quickly became a bastion of Christianity in Europe. The importance of Portugal and Spain would increase until they became the dominant powers of Europe in the 16th century.

However, the success in the West was not copied in the East. There was trouble in the Holy Land, and the 13th century was a period of lost opportunities and failed crusades. Moreover, a terrible force from the East was descending on the area, and a major military presence was growing in Africa that would threaten the existence of the Crusader States. It was a frustrating and anxious time for the warrior monks and their supporters. As the Templars gained honor and prestige in the Iberian Peninsula, they were steadily losing ground in Outremer until a tragic ending happened.

Chapter Nine – The Beginning of the End

"Death came among the proceeds from all sides and by all roads: we killed all that thou hast appointed to guard the city or defend its approaches."

-Babyars in a letter to Bohemond VI of Antioch

The Crusades lasted almost two hundred years and ended as dramatically as they began. There would be calls for crusades later, particularly after the fall of Constantinople in 1453, but not much came of those efforts. Europe was involved in other matters, and the major crusading powers, England and France, were locked in a contest called the Hundred Years' War. Their interest in anything that happened in the eastern Mediterranean significantly dropped since affairs closer to home drew the attention of the reigning dynasties.

The religious significance of the Crusades was fading. The Fourth Crusade was little more than a hostile takeover by Venice of one of its commercial rivals. Many people in Europe, particularly Italian merchants, seemed more interested in striking a separate deal with the Muslims than trying to present a united front for the sake of the Holy Land. Papal bulls and sermons tried to whip up a frenzy, but not much interest was forthcoming.

Frankly, Europe was getting tired of the whole idea. Few were interested in traveling a thousand miles from home to a sunbaked land where no one trusted anybody else. Besides, there were opportunities in eastern Europe, particularly Prussia and the Baltic region, where knights in the Crusades could gain the remission of sins while plundering the countryside.

The Templars were the predominant religious military order at one time, but they were starting to get some competition. The Knights Hospitaller were another significant order of knights, and the Spanish were creating their own bands of mounted warriors to carry the fight to the Muslims.

The Order of Brothers of the German House of Saint Mary in Jerusalem, commonly known as the Teutonic Knights, started by defending pilgrims in the Holy Land but later did exceptionally well commercially in the Baltic region. The younger sons of noble families sought opportunities with the Teutonic Knights without crossing continents.

The 13th century saw the Knights Templar slowly fade as a strategic military presence in the Middle East. The Templars were not yet done, but it was a new day and a new age. Their mission in Outremer shrank as the Crusader States became increasingly smaller.

New Ventures Elsewhere

The core business of the Knights Templar had been the defense of pilgrims going to the Holy Land. It did not mean they were unavailable elsewhere. Any crusade declared by the pope might justify Templars being sent to offer assistance, which was evident in the Reconquista. A curious situation for the Templars occurred in the Albigensian Crusade, which would have extreme repercussions later.

The Albigensian Crusade

Heresies and dissent plagued the Roman Catholic Church throughout the Middle Ages. Moreover, Europe's intellectual and theological developments often resulted in local sects at loggerheads with the establishment.

The Catholic Church was a substantial bureaucracy throughout the medieval world. It was the primary mover of education, and universities were established by monastic orders and prelates throughout the centuries. However, the church was more than that. It was also the social welfare agency for Europe, a substantial patron of the arts, and the founder of hospitals. Monasteries were economic centers in rural regions. It cannot be denied that the Catholic Church provided essential social services and worked to improve society.

Unfortunately, it was extremely powerful, and power can breed corruption. Consequently, the church was routinely criticized by those wishing to reform it and return it to its commitment to the poor and disadvantaged.

A significant heresy grew in southern France called Catharism. The Cathars rejected the need for an established clergy and liturgical hierarchy. Instead, they believed that each person had an individual connection with God and could communicate directly through prayer.

Some of their beliefs drew from earlier heresies and made these people a severe threat to the established order. For example, Cathars believed in the duality of the universe. This was a creed that was propagated by the Gnostics centuries before and was centered on the idea that a universe of darkness clashed with a universe of light. The physical world was full of corruption, and sin was controlled by evil. The pure spiritual world was the realm of God. The Cathars looked at the Roman Catholic Church and all of its wealth and the corruption of some of the clergy. They concluded that the church was an advocate for evil.

Catharism had a broad appeal and was especially prominent in the Languedoc area of France. The number of people who converted to Catharism was so alarming that Pope Innocent III called for a crusade in 1209 against this religious minority. The result was a campaign of ethnic cleansing, and thousands of Cathars were killed.

The Cathars and the Templars

The Cathars were perceived as a threat to the social order of the 13th century, but the ordinary folks were not the only adherents. The French aristocracy of southern France did not appreciate the Catholic clergy's authority in the area. Beneath the surface was a power struggle between French nobles and French prelates. As a result, there were members of the aristocracy who sided with the Cathars. Some of those aristocrats had connections to the Templars either as benefactors or relatives.

The order tried to stay neutral in this conflict. They did not want to alienate those who gave them financial support. There have been suggestions that many Templars agreed with the Cathars on several theological issues. This is the stuff of legends and fiction today, but back then, this assumed association was a source of trouble. The Templars would later pay dearly for what was perceived as a close connection to heretics.[38]

The Mongols and the Templars

The middle of the 13th century saw a new world order suddenly come crashing into the societies of the Middle East. The Mongol Empire spread far and fast from its origins in Mongolia, defeating and destroying cultures that got in its way. A major shock to the Islamic world occurred when the Mongols seized and sacked Baghdad in 1258. The Abbasid dynasty, which had ruled for five hundred years, came to an end with the last caliph being killed by the invaders.

The Christians tried to create an alliance with the Asian intruders but were rebuffed. The Mongols had other things in mind. The Templars were uneasy about this new presence. The twentieth grand master, Thomas Bérard, lobbied strongly for a united front where all Christians forgot their differences to face a common and severe threat.

The Mongols were not limited to attacking the Middle East. Mongol forces under the command of Batu Khan and Subutai invaded Hungary after the Hungarians refused to surrender refugees who had fled the Mongol advance. One of the battles fought between the Christian armies and the Mongols was at Liegnitz (modern-day Legnica, Poland) on April 9th, 1241. The Templars were among the participants.

The Mongols' primary strategy was to feign a retreat, draw their opponents into a hot pursuit that separated the cavalry from the infantry, and then turn around and counterattack viciously. That tactic was successfully employed at Liegnitz. The Mongols drew the Christian cavalry away from the main body of troops and used a smokescreen to confuse the pursuing knights. The Mongol counterattack decimated the European ranks.

The Templars allegedly came close to killing Batu, with the Mongol general only being saved by the actions of his bodyguard. We cannot say for sure this happened, but Templar Grand Master Ponce d'Aubon reported to King Louis IX of France that the Templars suffered significant losses in the battle. The event that stopped the Mongols from proceeding farther into Europe was the death of Grand Khan Ögedei.[39]

---

[38] McMahon, T. (2013, December 30). *Knights Templar Links to the Cathar Heresy.* Retrieved from thetemplarknight.com: https://thetemplarknight.com/2013/12/30/knights-templar-cathars/.
[39] Timenote.info. (2023, February 23). *First Mongol Invasion of Poland; Battle of Legnica.*

The Mongol threat to the Middle East was substantial, and it compelled the Crusader States to make a decision that ultimately contributed to their destruction and the complete collapse of Outremer.

The Decline of Outremer

Frederick II left the Kingdom of Jerusalem in better shape than when he had found it. The Crusader States were in reasonably good condition, and what was needed was a unity of purpose like the First Crusade. However, that did not happen.

The Christian rulers failed to recognize that their strength was in solidarity. Instead, they quarreled amongst each other with different agendas and had one group fighting another. The War of the Lombards (1228–1243) saw the Kingdom of Jerusalem fighting the Kingdom of Cyprus. Although the Barons' Crusade (1239–1241) saw the Kingdom of Jerusalem become as large as it was before the fall of Jerusalem in 1187, that prominence did not last very long. Jerusalem fell once again, this time to the Khwarazmians, in 1244. As if all of this was not bad enough, Genoa and Venice fought a war over commercial interests in Acre (the War of Saint Sabas, 1256–1268).[40]

The chaos of the 13th century was affecting the ability of the Knights Templar to concentrate on their mission of protecting pilgrims. More importantly, the order was on the defensive, as were all the other knights in the area. A significant engagement was the Battle of La Forbie in 1244. Only thirty-three Templars survived the battle. It was a dark time for the Knights Templar, and it would only get worse. Another charismatic and ruthless leader was rising up in Egypt.

Enter Babyars

The Mamluks were enslaved people who knew how to fight. They hold the distinction of being one of the few warriors who successfully fought and routed the Mongols. They overthrew the Ayyubid dynasty in Egypt in 1250 and were the preeminent Islamic power in the region.

They were religious fanatics, which made them dangerous. They were not interested in commercial enterprises but in strict adherence to the Quran and victory on the battlefield. Their relationship with the

---

Retrieved from timenote.info: https://timenote.info/en/events/First-Mongol-invasion-of-Poland-Battle-of-Legnica .

[40] History-Maps.com. (2023, February 23). *1099-1291 Crusader States (Outremer).* Retrieved from history-maps.com: https://history-maps.com/story/Crusader-States-Outremer.

Crusader States was treacherous, to say the least. The Mamluks had no problem breaking truces, ignoring the conventional rules of war, and slaughtering prisoners. They appeared to be more interested in annihilation than the accumulation of assets.[41]

His full name was al-Malik al-Zahir Rukn al-Din Babyars al-Bunduqdari. He is known to history as Babyars (also sometimes spelled Baibars) and was the sultan of Egypt and Syria from 1260 to 1277. Babyars has a folk hero status among many Arabs, and stories of his life are immensely popular. However, he was the worst nightmare the Knights Templar had ever faced.

Babyars wanted to be like Saladin, but there were some significant differences between the two. Saladin was known for his empathy and chivalrous nature; Babyars was ruthless. He was a vicious fighter and had little mercy for anybody. He wanted to see an end to the Crusader States, and he very nearly succeeded.

An example of his ruthless behavior can be found in a letter he sent to the prince of Antioch when the Mamluks took the city in 1268. Babyars showed no mercy and slaughtered nearly thirty-three thousand people and enslaved thousands more. The sultan openly bragged about what he did, and the letter to Bohemond VI included the following:

"If thou hast seen by palaces given up to the flames, the dead devoured by the fire of this world, the Church of St. Paul and that of St. Peter completely and entirely destroyed, certainly thou wouldst of cried out Would to heaven that I were become dust!"[42]

Babyars had heavy cavalry and wasn't afraid of Christian knights in armor. So, he began a full-scale attack on Outremer in 1265 by attacking and destroying Caesarea. Although he initially bypassed the Templar stronghold of Château Pèlerin, he attacked settlements nearby and destroyed anything in his way. He finally turned his attention to the Templar castle at Safad.

[41] Dr. Schrader, P. (2023, February 22). *The Decline and Fall of the Crusader States in the 13th Century.* Retrieved from defendingcrusaderkingdoms.blogspot.com: http://defendingcrusaderkingdoms.blogspot.com/2021/02/the-decline-and-fall-of-crusader-states.html .

[42] Ballandalus.com. (2014, February 1). *Conquest of Antioch (1268): Letter of Babyars (d.1277) to Bohemond VI (d.1275).* Retrieved from ballandalus.wordpress.com: https://ballandalus.wordpress.com/2014/02/01/conquest-of-antioch-1268-letter-of-baybars-d-1277-to-bohemond-vi-d-1275/ .

Safad was well garrisoned and well supplied. Babyars originally offered easy terms to the defenders if they surrendered, but his gifts were rejected by being tossed over the battlements. Enraged, the sultan attacked with siege towers, dug mines, and used Greek fire on the walls. His efforts were not successful, so Babyars turned to treachery.

He convinced the Syrians who were part of the garrison that they would receive safe conduct if the citadel surrendered. It caused dissension in the ranks, and he fooled the garrison into thinking they would receive what he had promised. The gates of Safed were opened, and the Templars marched out, assuming they would have safe conduct to Acre. Instead, they were massacred by the Mamluks. Babyars continued to attack Templar strongholds and menace the Crusader kingdoms until he finally died by accidentally drinking a cup of poison he intended for one of his dinner guests.[43]

The lack of reinforcements from the West and an inability to successfully ward off the Mamluks were taking their toll. The climax was approaching, and the scene of the last stand of the Templars was at Acre.

The Last Stand in Outremer

Babyars wreaked havoc on the Crusader States, and his successors kept up the pace. The goal of the Mamluk sultanate was to end the presence of the Christians in the Levant, and they systematically leveled castles and seized towns in Outremer. The Knights Templar and the other fighting orders kept up the resistance, but their efforts were not working. Western Europe was no longer interested in Palestine, and the crusading passion of years past had evaporated. The County of Tripoli fell to the Mamluks in 1289, and only Acre was left.

However, Acre was not an easy target. It was a major port and could easily be resupplied by sea. King Edward I of England provided the necessary money to refurbish its defenses, and the Knights Templar and the Knights Hospitaller were prominent parts of the garrison. The Mamluks looked for an excuse to take Acre and finally got the opportunity when several Muslim merchants were killed in 1290.

Sultan Qalawun demanded reparations and rejected the offer made by the Crusaders. The sultan raised a large army, which he claimed was going to be used against adversaries in Africa. The Templar grand master

[43] Jones, D. (2017). *The Templars: The Rise and Spectacular Fall of God's Holy Warriors.*

in Acre, William of Beaujeu, discovered Qalawun's real intention was to attack Acre and warned the city of what was being planned. Qalawun died, and his son, al-Sharaf, ignored all diplomatic efforts to maintain peace. On April 5th, 1291, a large Mamluk army began taking offensive positions around the city. The estimates for the number of Muslim combatants were possibly exaggerated, but it is safe to say that its size was many times that of the garrison defending Acre.

The composition of the defenders gives an idea of how commercial interests had replaced religious idealism by this time. The Venetians and Pisans were ready to defend the walls, but the Genoese, who negotiated a separate peace, evacuated and sailed off to Cyprus. What was left to defend Acre was a garrison estimated to be approximately six hundred knights and thirteen thousand infantry.

The Mamluks put up their siege engines and began the task of destroying Acre's defenses. Sorties led by William of Beaujeu and later by the Hospitallers did nothing to relieve the pressure being placed on the city. The king of Cyprus and Jerusalem, Henry II, arrived on May 4th with reinforcements. Unfortunately, there were too few to make any difference. Further attempts at negotiation were rejected by al-Sharaf, who sensed that victory was close at hand.

Mamluk miners brought down a significant tower on May 18th, forcing the garrison to retreat to the old city's walls. The fighting was fierce but futile; the Mamluks were gaining control of the situation. Henry II abandoned the city at this point and returned to Cyprus. Grand Master Beaujeu fell defending a breach in the walls.

The situation was hopeless, and the senior Templar in Acre at the time, Peter de Sevrey, realized that further resistance would not be productive. He negotiated a surrender on May 25th with honorable terms. The truce would allow the surviving garrison and all women and children to depart in exchange for surrendering the remaining defenses.

However, those conditions were not met, as the Mamluk troops went on a rampage of slaughter. De Sevrey was killed, but not before he ordered the Templar commander, Thibauld Gaudin, to escape with the Templar treasure to Sidon. On May 28th, the eastern wall of the Templar fortifications was undermined and collapsed. Acre was now in the hands of the Mamluks.

The Final Story

Some Christian enclaves were left in Outremer, but it was over for the Crusaders. Beirut fell on May 31st, and what remained of the Templar presence–Sidon, Tortosa, and Atlit–were evacuated by August 14th, 1291. After that, there was nothing left to fight for, and no crusading army was sailing in over the horizon.

What was left of the Templar contingent sailed from the shores of Palestine to the island of Cyprus. They still had properties there, but there was no serious chance of the knights ever returning. The remaining warrior monks no doubt looked back in sadness as their ships sailed west. They did not know this at the time, but they were sailing into hell.[44]

[44] Schrader, H. P. (2023, February 24). *The Knights Templar and the Fall of Acre 1291.* Retrieved from defenderofjerusalem.com: https://www.defenderofjerusalem.com/kt--acre.html.

Chapter Ten – Financing the Enterprise

"Money deposited with the Templars was not pooled and reinvested, but remained in its owners strong boxes within the Order's treasury and cannot be accessed without the owner's permission."

-Helen Nicholson, The Knights Templar: A New History

Medieval warfare was expensive. Furnishing knights with horses and armor was just one cost. Men at arms, archers, light auxiliaries, and other footmen needed to be paid and equipped. Human resources aside, there are also practical considerations, such as building siege engines and moving an entire army distances of up to one hundred miles or more. And this is all in addition to building fortifications that could withstand lengthy sieges, which meant not just the structure of a castle but also the provisioning of the garrison within. Money was always an issue.

The Templars could not rely on donations alone. Those are one-time contributions that provide an infusion of cash for a short period of time. Once the money was spent, the donor had to be approached again, or other donors had to be found. The Templar mission was not a one-project-at-a-time operation but an ongoing commitment to providing protective services.

What was needed was evergreen funding, a type of financing that is gradual and ongoing. If the Templars were able to create a structure where there was a steady and consistent cash flow, they would be more successful. So, that is what the order did.

Capitalizing on the Image

Modern marketing techniques often rely on the opinion of focus groups and surveys and how to promote a brand. There is no way the Templar founders had any access to these sources of information. Nevertheless, they achieved results that mirror a modern company.

The Templar image was one of a chaste knight protecting innocent and virtuous pilgrims on their way to the Holy Land. That starkly contrasts with the way most knights in the Middle Ages behaved. Chivalry was essentially a poetic device used by troubadours to entertain the ladies. History suggests that many knights in shining armor were actually thugs looking for loot and doing the bidding of their lords. Templars and other warrior monks of the age seemed to closely personify the perfect gentleman that the code of chivalry was trying to project. What they were doing was for the greater glory of God, not for personal advancement.

Protecting the Aristocratic Brand

Medieval Europe was a violent place. There were huge wars, and there were also local feuds going on almost everywhere. The ruling class did not tolerate dissent, and problem-makers were often ruthlessly eliminated. Attempts to project chivalrous or high-minded images were clouded by atrocious acts. Richard the Lionheart was considered an honorable man, but he still ordered the deaths of thousands of hostages. Edward the Black Prince was commended for his modesty and courtesy. Yet he ordered the destruction of Limoges in France. The imagery of chivalry was often tarnished by reality.

Nevertheless, the aristocracy tried to appear pious and virtuous, which explains why they endowed monasteries and built hospitals. Acts of religious devotion were encouraged, even though the actor could, at times, be vicious and insensitive. Donating to the Knights Templar proved that a noble was interested in protecting Christianity and the Holy Land. The contributions might also take the place of going on a crusade.

The Structure

Donations to the Templars did not only come in cash. The order also received tracts of land and other properties that were potentially lucrative. For example, kings during the Reconquista gave old Muslim fortifications to the Templars, which was sensible because it meant the rulers did not have to raise garrisons or maintain those forts; the Templars took care of both and contributed significantly to defense. It would have been easy for the order to sell donated land, but they would do more than barter in real estate.

Still, the foundation of what would grow to be the Templars' incredible wealth was land. Land provided opportunities for the order to do more than rely on occasional donations from a feudal lord. If managed properly, the Templars could own fertile places that provided economic opportunities. But, of course, they had to be managed.

The Commanderies

The commanderies were the administrative hubs of the Templars, and they were located in western Europe. Basically, a commandery consisted of a group of buildings that were more than armories or military supply depots. The facilities included mills, presses, and other structures where useful work would be done.

Commanderies were organized into dormitories, chapels, chapter house refractories, and buildings primarily concerned with farming and managing the land. The knights themselves were drawn from the aristocracy, but nobles were not tillers of the field and did not know much about how to operate a farm.

So, those Templars, who were essentially noncombatants, happened to be drawn from peasant stock and were sergeants. To differentiate them from the purely military members of the order, these Templars were called the black brothers, and those who came from aristocracy were called white brothers. The number of commanderies grew significantly over the years. It is estimated that nearly a thousand could be found all over Europe.[45]

Sergeants

The popular image of Templars is one of mounted warriors charging into battle with swords and shields. Unfortunately, that image is not closely related to reality at all. In fact, it is estimated that only one in ten Templars were knights. Most of them were sergeants, and while they did fight as light cavalry, most of them were trained in useful trades, such as building, blacksmithing, and administration.

[45] Templars-route.eu. (2023, February 26). *Templar Heritage in France*. Retrieved from templars-route.eu: https://www.templars-route.eu/en/templar-heritage-in-france/ .

Those connected to the farms were under the jurisdiction of the Commanders of Lands and took care of the maintenance and operation of Templar estates. The sergeants were easily distinguished from the knights because they wore a black tunic with a black or brown mantle. They did have the red cross of the Templars on their uniforms.[46]

An interesting distinction between the knights and the sergeants is that while the knights swore formal vows, the sergeants did not. Instead, sergeants were bound to a commitment to service. This means their obligations were defined in a contract for a fixed term. It gives us the impression that they were contract workers, but there seems to be little doubt that they were as loyal to the order as any knight.[47] There were sergeants at arms, who were available for combat, and sergeants at service, who were noncombatants and held primarily administrative positions.

Land Management

There were various reasons for granting land to the Templars. The original grants in Provence, a region in France, were intended to provide supplies for action in the Holy Land. However, in Catalonia, the intent was to draw the Templars into the Reconquista by giving them frontier castles that could be used to defend Spanish territory from the Muslims. And other donations of territory were to be used for the order's livelihood. Whatever the intention, the Templars rapidly became sizable landlords in Europe.[48] Estate centers were called preceptories, which were where agricultural activities were concentrated.

An excellent example of how Templars managed their land was in England and Wales. By the start of the 14th century, the Knights Templar was among the largest estate holders in England. Their rural properties were one of the more significant producers of dairy products and raw

---

[46] Medieval Warfare.info. (2023, February 26). *Monastic Orders Knights Templar, Knights Hospitaller and Others.* Retrieved from medievalwarfare.info: https://www.medievalwarfare.info/templars.htm#:~:text=Sergeants.,cavalry%20with%20a%20single%20horse.

[47] Knightstemplarorder.org. (2023, February 28). *Authentic Templar Banking Principles. Original Biblical Banking Practices of the Knights Templar.* Retrieved from knightstemplar.org: https://knightstemplarorder.org/heritage/templar-banking/.

[48] Forey, A. (2021, March 18). *Early Templar Administration in Provence and North-Eastern Spain.* Retrieved from journals.openedition.org: https://journals.openedition.org/medievalista/4484?lang=en.

wool.[49]

Historians have tried to discover the Templars' role in rural England in the Middle Ages. Calculations suggest that by 1308, the time when the Knights Templar had dissolved in England, the Templars owned more than 300,000 sheep that produced 39,000 pounds of wool annually. In addition, records show that the Templars used the best agricultural practices of the time. For example, evidence compiled in Lincolnshire indicates the order made extensive use of fertilizer, multiple plowing techniques, weeding, manipulation of the sowing rate, and efficient animal husbandry.

Property ownership was apparent in the urban areas of Europe. Today, prime real estate is the source of income and wealth for many investors. It was the same for the Templars one thousand years ago. They held property in urban locations, most importantly the Atlantic and Channel coast ports and Italian cities, such as Lucca, Pisa, Venice, Florence, and Siena.

Geoffrey FitzStephen, the grand master of the Knights Templar in England, requested an Inquest of Lands in 1185 that produced a record of donors of land, tenants, and the rents and services owed to the order. While the written record still needs to be researched, what we know about Templar activity in England is impressive. The Charter, Close, and Patent Rolls indicate how the Templars further developed the property holdings. It seems clear that land was not allowed to remain idle, either in the countryside or in the towns.

Urban Property Owners

Medieval historians admit that the Roman Catholic Church was instrumental in helping develop English towns. The abbeys and the cathedrals were more than reliquaries. They were sources of employment for the local population and encouraged market commerce. The Templars, as a warrior monastic order, contributed as well.

While less successful than the monasteries or pilgrim sites, the Templars were involved in creating planned settlements and cooperating with aristocratic investors in places like Bristol. In addition, the Templars were involved in urban development in areas like Baldock.

---

[49] Slavin, P. (2014, February 19). *The Templars' Land.* Retrieved from medieval.eu: https://www.medieval.eu/knights-templars-land/.

The Templars received market privileges as one form of donation. Markets and yearly fairs were granted to them. In addition, the Templars received income from the stalls they rented out at the marketplaces, and they also collected rents from tenants for lodging or doing business in buildings owned by the Templars.

The towns that were created in part by Templar activity were ordinarily within easy traveling distance of a preceptory, allowing the Templars to use fairs to sell produce from their farms. Templars also provided other services, such as hauling grain to market. The Templars' commercial activity was not as great as other monastic orders. However, local markets benefited from the presence of a nearby preceptory, which was made available for commercial use by the order. Templar chapels provided necessary social services as well as the expected religious services.

The Knights Templar had a noticeable impact on urban life in England, and it was not the only European country that benefited from the order's presence.

The presence of the Knights Templar gradually shrank in the Holy Land as military setbacks in Outremer became commonplace. Nevertheless, the Knights Templar was established in Europe's rural and urban communities. Although the order took resources to be used in various military campaigns, it can be justifiably stated the Knights Templar gave more back to the local economy than it took. The Templars were certainly not parasites.[50]

We do not ordinarily associate land management and rural/urban development with Templar non-military activities. However, the order's contribution to European society and commerce extended into other areas. The most significant was in finance. Templars perfected ways to raise money for projects. These knights also created a system of moving money that was almost unheard of at the time. Some of the financial transactions that modern businesses take for granted had their origins in the commanderies and preceptories of the order.

---

[50] Lee, J. S. (2022, March 11). *The Knights Templar in English Towns.* Retrieved from cambridge.org: https://www.cambridge.org/core/journals/urban-history/article/knights-templar-in-english-towns/1EB941BD556C016793A6B83499ABC110.

Templars and Medieval Banking

Financial transactions in the Middle Ages were cash-only affairs. You had to have the money in your hand to purchase anything. That was not a problem at a local market or a pilgrimage center that was not far away. However, it got more challenging if the transaction occurred hundreds of miles away from home. The farther a person was away from where they lived, the greater their chance of being robbed.

This grave danger was something that pilgrims were forced to deal with. Traveling to Jerusalem could take weeks or even months, and a pilgrim was at the mercy of the highway and the sea routes. Moreover, bandits could be Christian or Muslim, and they were inclined to kill a victim after robbing them of all their wealth.

The Knights Templar was originally founded to protect pilgrims, but it was impossible to guard every group making its way to a sacred spot. There needed to be a way to allow these travelers to journey with as little cash as possible. Remarkably, the Templars came up with a solution.

Letters of Credit

A pilgrim was a fat duck waiting to be plucked. The Templars devised a solution that would lighten the travelers' burdens. These were letters of credit.

The process was brilliantly simple. Pilgrims could deposit their money at a Templar commandery or preceptory and receive a letter of credit from the Templars, including the amount deposited. Then, after having arrived at their destination in Outremer, they would go to the nearest Templar establishment and get that same amount by showing their letter of credit (Templars would adjust the amount for currency conversion). Of course, robbers were looking for all that glitters. A letter of credit did not look like gold, even though it gave the bearer access to that. So, pilgrimages became a lot safer, not just because there might be an armed escort but also because the pilgrims were not carrying any cash on them.

Templars did a lot of traveling to protect pilgrim bands, and they could transport money from one Templar outpost to another. The number of Templar establishments significantly expanded all over Europe and the Middle East from the 12th to the 14th century. Those places could be considered branch offices.[51]

---

[51] DefendersofJerusalem.com. (2023, February 28). *The Money-Lenders in the Temple: The*

Templar Banking Practices

The Templars followed a primary philosophy to govern all of their banking: All financial services of the Templar Order must be dedicated to promoting a spiritual economy under God's natural law as common law instead of a secular economy under parliamentary laws as statutory law.

Templars used sovereign coins, which were religious coins that represented moral currency or moral value, as a medium of exchange. These had earned merit under God's law. This was in contrast to secular coins that were used for commercial goods and services under governmental law.

The pope gave the Templar Order certain rights and privileges, including being responsible only to the pope, which would help enormously in any financial activity. Here are some of the banking practices that were common within the Templar finance structure.

- Traveler's Checks and Bonds

  The basic concept has already been mentioned. It was possible for a person to deposit money in one European city and then travel to another place in Europe to withdraw the money. A handling fee was charged for this. Transferable banknotes were developed that used medieval common law principles.

- Common Law Trust

  The Templars created an infrastructure for sovereign wealth management. Nobles could place not only money but also their estates, assets, and other valuables under the control of the Templars for security. A power of attorney placed those assets in management under a deed of trust advances that would be reclaimed on a person's return. Beneficiaries would include the family of a noble and would guarantee those assets were given to the beneficiaries or to the church if the original owner perished.

- Safety Deposit Boxes

  The Templars kept safe boxes and secure facilities within their establishments. Anyone could safely store substantial amounts of treasures there.

Banking Activities of the Knights Templar. Retrieved from defendersofJerusalem.com: https://www.defenderofjerusalem.com/templar-banking-activities.html.

- No-interest Loans

  This Templar service helped develop European economies by introducing loans given by the order based on the liquidity of the Templars. This practice came close to violating the biblical prohibition of usury, which was a standard policy of the Roman Catholic Church at the time. However, the Templars found a way to get around that.

  These loans were made on the security of income from the borrower's land or estate. The Templars did not take real estate as collateral but retained the rights to revenues generated by the property. The borrower kept the real estate.

Other financial practices originated with the Templars and, over the years, became the standard way of doing business in the financial world. All of this made the Knights Templar a primary player in the economies of western Europe.[52]

Money Managers to the Crown

The papal bull *Omne datum optimum* did more than exempt the Templars from paying tithes; it also permitted them to collect tithes. King Henry II of England gave the Templars responsibility for managing the Saladin tithe, and Templars played a role in collecting money for later crusades. The order became indispensable to various Christian monarchs regarding money matters.

The Templars did not just collect crusade money. They also provided loans to the rulers of Europe. Louis IX was forced to ask the Templars for a loan to pay the remaining amount owed on his ransom. King John of England needed money to pay his soldiers and turned to the Templars for the required cash. They did not charge interest on the loans but requested payment for administration and other expenses. This included a sizable fee for a loan to King Edward I of England. Popes also needed cash; Pope Alexander III borrowed heavily from the Templars to stay financially solvent.

What helped the Templars was their recordkeeping. Financial transactions were meticulously recorded; major customers, including Queen Mother Blanche of Castile, received detailed accounts of their

[52] Knightstemplarorder.org. (2023, February 28). *Authentic Templar Banking Principles. Original Biblical Banking Practices of the Knights Templar.*

dealings with the order. These records were important whenever there was a dispute over money issues. As a result, the order was western Europe's principal international banking establishment by the end of the 13th century.[53]

The financial prowess of the Knights Templar did not happen overnight. It took two centuries for these warrior monks' economic and financial power to grow. Naturally, there were setbacks and mistakes along the way, but gradually, the order grew into an even greater force in banking than it ever did on the battlefield. It drew the attention of many people.

But it also created envy. The Templars were better at gathering and using money than most governments in Europe during the Middle Ages. The order's power and wealth were very noticeable. And the riches of the Knights Templar came into view of a fair-haired monarch who saw an opportunity to gain possession of what the Templars had worked so hard to achieve.

---

[53] Bustani, H. A. (2023, February 28). *Templar Banking: How to Go from Donated Rags to Vast Riches.* Retrieved from medievalists.net: https://www.medievalists.net/2021/08/templar-banking/ .

Chapter Eleven – Disaster

"I beseech you to turn my face towards the Virgin Mary, of whom our Lord Christ was born."

-Last words of Jacques DeMolay

The loss of Acre was a tragedy, but it was not disastrous for the Templars. The last Templar stronghold in the Levant, Ruad, was taken by the Mamluks in 1302, ending the Templars' presence in the Holy Land. The order, however, was still a potent force.

After all, it was the financial juggernaut of the Late Middle Ages. Templar commanderies and preceptories owned significant estates and properties. The Templar presence in western Europe was a financial network that did not collapse with the retreat from the Middle East. Everything was still intact, and the Templars had the money to organize and implement another crusade. They remained a force to be reckoned with at the dawn of the 14th century.

Remarkably, the Order of the Knights Templar was destroyed within a few years and was officially suppressed on March 22nd, 1312. This sudden and definitive fall of the warrior monks was the result of incredible royal treachery.

Philip the Fair

King Philip IV of France was the primary agent of the order's demise. Philip was an aggressive and ambitious king who engaged in wars to increase the size of his kingdom and his power. Wars cost money, and Philip drove France into financial straits. The French king was aware of the financial resources of the Templars and how these knights could solve his money problems. Philip did not want to make financial arrangements with the Knights Templar, though; he wanted all of their treasure and was ruthless enough to destroy the Templars to get it.

Partners in Crime

Prior events helped Philip execute what he planned for the Templars. The French king had been feuding with Pope Boniface VIII over the right to tax church property, and the quarrel quickly escalated. As a result, the pope was kidnapped by Philip and died within a month. His successor lasted no more than a year; it is rumored that he was poisoned.

Philip wanted to make sure that the papacy was in his pocket. Consequently, he manipulated the College of Cardinals, which elected Philip's candidate, Bertrand de Goth, as pope. De Goth took the official name of Clement V. Philip wanted his puppet to be close at hand and convinced (or pressured) Clement to move the Holy See to Avignon, France (beginning what is referred to as the Babylonian captivity of the papacy). The French king was better able to keep an eye on the pope and exert further pressure on the man. Clement V proved to be a timid and accommodating man who quickly gave in to whatever Philip wanted.[54]

Philip was aided in his conspiracy against the Templars by his lawyer and advisor, Guillaume de Nogaret, and his chamberlain, Enguerrand de Marigny. The French monarch began to set his sights on the unsuspecting Knights Templar.

A Business Association

The Templars had little reason to suspect what would happen to them. They had a relationship with the French monarchy. The Templars were authorized to manage various financial functions within France and were also Philip's primary creditor. The order financed Philips's wars and provided money for his sister's dowry. Indeed, the Templars protected Philip from an insurrection that occurred in Paris after the king had debased the currency. It did not seem possible that Philip would betray them.

---

[54] Kannon, C. H. (2023, March 2). *King Phillip IV, Pope Clement V, and the Fall of the Knights Templar.* Retrieved from view.officeapps.live.com: https://view.officeapps.live.com/op/view.aspx?src=http%3A%2F%2Fplaza.ufl.edu%2Fandrei.gandila%2FPhillip%2520IV_Templars.doc&wdOrigin=BROWSELINK.

Unfortunately, the Templars were not watching their client closely. Philip had a reputation for seizing property whenever he needed it and had done so with the Lombard bankers and the Jews. He was aware of the overall value of the Templars, and he wanted all that the knights had. So, he schemed with his counselors on how to get it.

An Unsuspecting Grand Master

Jacques de Molay was the grand master of the Templars in the early years of the 14th century. He was elected to the position shortly after the fall of Acre and wanted to return to the Holy Land and regain lost territories. He spent years trying to get the needed support and coordination for this effort. He was also a reformer who wanted to make improvements within the order. In 1305, he was asked by Clement V to make some recommendations about the new crusade and possible changes within the Templar Order.

On June 6th, 1306, de Molay and the grand master of the Hospitallers were invited to a conference with Pope Clement to discuss the issues. De Molay was in France in early 1307 and was still there when the trap was sprung.

Friday the 13th

Neither Philip nor Nogaret can be accused of having scruples or ethics. They were determined to get what they wanted, and they were not going to let integrity get in the way. They compiled a list of accusations to justify the arrest and seizure of Templars. Some of the more salacious charges include the following:

- New members of the order were required to deny Christ, the Virgin Mary, and all the saints.
- Templars said Christ was a false prophet, and no one who believed in him could receive salvation.
- Knights were ordered to spit on a crucifix.
- The order worshiped a head of some description that may be an idol called Baphomet.
- New members were kissed on the mouth, navel, stomach, buttocks, and spine. Same-sex relationships were encouraged.

- The Knights Templar rejected the sacraments.[55]

Sometimes, the death of a thousand cuts is preceded by a thousand whispers. Rumors had persisted through the years that the Knights Templar and the Cathars had a close relationship. This association with such a dangerous heresy was fuel for the fire. Some of the accusations made against the knights reflected the ideas of the Cathars. However, the connection between the two groups was part of a disinformation campaign to encourage people to believe the Templars were anti-Christian.

There would be over one hundred accusations levied against the Knights Templar. The intent was to convince people that the Templars were heretics and grave sinners. Furthermore, it would simplify the dissolution of the order and seize all of its assets. What was necessary was to pin the Templars to one or more of these accusations. The judicial process of the time would then fall into place, and a guilty verdict would be assured.

It would take a lot of work to take down the order, though. The knights were not concentrated in one place, and the final assault would have to be well coordinated. It undoubtedly took a lot of intricate planning to do the deed, but Philip and his advisors created a successful course of action.

On October 13th, 1307, the French king succeeded in having hundreds of Templars in France arrested. They were turned over to the Inquisition, and all the Templar property in France was confiscated. Philip perpetrated a fraud that was phenomenally successful in its first stages.

Interrogations and Torture

The knights were trained to be ready to endure torture at the hands of their captors. Each knew it was possible that Muslims could seize them and that they would likely be physically abused to break their spirits. They were undoubtedly amazed that they would have to use their training to endure torture by fellow Christians.

---

[55] McMahon, T. (2017, October 3). *Ten Accusations Made against the Knights Templar.* Retrieved from thetemplarknight.com: https://thetemplarknight.com/2017/10/03/knights-templar-accusations/.

Interrogations in the Middle Ages were not pleasant. The intent was to break the captive physically so that a confession, no matter how fantastic, was pulled from them and later used as evidence in court. Even the grand master was tortured. Nobody was going to be spared.

What these men endured would make a horror movie look like a comedy. The rack was used, and there were other devices as well, such as tying the victim's hands behind his back, fastening heavy weights to the feet, hoisting the man in the air, and suddenly dropping him to the ground. Teeth were drawn, and their feet were roasted. The heels of a knight would be enclosed in an iron heel, and then the device was tightened for maximum pain. Fingers were broken. In addition, the captive Templars were subjected to near starvation and cold.[56]

It is no wonder that many Templars confessed to what they knew were outrageous accusations. There is only so much pain that a human being can endure, and those abused men could take no more.

The Trials and Tribulations

The Templars were forced to go through the farce of a trial. Accounts from the Stalinist era of Russia showed that such trials were public plays that exaggerated the accused's guilt and made them look like monsters. The verdict was in before the judges sat on the bench.

Nevertheless, Philip IV needed a formal procedure to justify his actions and to give official approval of his intentions. First, the Templars had to be proven to be heretics guilty of horrific crimes. The trial in Paris ran from October 19th to November 24th, 1307, with 138 prisoners before the bench. Another trial was held at Poitiers between June 28th and July 2nd, 1308, where fifty-four Templars were tried.

We must remember that these men were viciously tortured and could expect further physical pain if they did not perform according to the script. The defendants admitted they were guilty of at least one of the charges. Ironically, their statements also admitted that the confessions were not derived from torture. This was only round one of the Templars in court.

In 1310, several Templars recanted their statements and were prepared to defend the order. However, this time, things were a little bit

---

[56] Knightstemplarvault.com. (2023, March 3). *Medieval Torture Methods Applied to the Knights Templar*. Retrieved from knightstemplarvault.com: https://knightstemplarvault.com/medieval-torture/ .

different. Pierre de Bologna, a Templar who was trained as a canon lawyer, represented the order in front of a papal commission in Rome. Pierre went before the bench and demanded a full disclosure of the accusers and all the information and evidence that had been gathered. The lawyer was not going to allow his clients to be destroyed by gossip and innuendo.

In May 1310, Philip de Marigny, Archbishop of Sens, took over the legal proceedings. (Interestingly, the archbishop was the half-brother of Enguerrand de Marigny.) The archbishop continued the proceedings for years, and there was no indication that he would be fair or impartial. The man knew the outcome that Philip IV wanted.

However, Clement V was finally developing some courage and insisted actual trials, not kangaroo courts, be used. Unfortunately, Philip wanted to prevent the Templars' witnesses from participating in the proceedings. As a result, fifty-four Templars were burned as heretics. The papal commission met again on November 3rd, 1310, and discovered the Templars had no defenders. Moreover, their defense attorney, Pierre de Bologna, had been arrested and forced to appear before Philip de Marigny. As a result, he was no longer available to plead the Templars' case.

Official Suppression

The Council of Vienne was an ecumenical council that met in Vienne, France, between 1311 and 1312. One piece of business before the council was the formal suppression of the Knights Templar. Included in the discussion was whether the lands owned by the Templars could be seized. The council initially believed that the order should have the right to defend itself and that there was no sufficient proof to convict the Knights Templar of heresy. However, their opinions changed when Philip IV himself appeared on March 20th, 1312.

The delegates cracked under the direct pressure of the French king. On March 22nd, 1312, Clement issued a papal bull, *Vox in excelso,* that officially suppressed the Order of the Templars. The pope went a step further on May 1312 with another bull, *Ad providam,* that transferred the assets of the Knights Templar to the Knights Hospitaller.

The defense of the Templars began to fall like a house of cards. Philip received a portion of the Templar assets in France to compensate for all the expenses. Other monarchs wanted their piece of the pie. Others tried to help the Templars. James II of Aragon defended the

Templars in his land. Although they were found innocent, the papal ban still applied to them. James insisted that the Templar property be given to the Order of Calatrava. A further series of papal bulls defined how the rest of the Templar assets would be distributed.

Other Templar trials were held throughout Europe, including Cyprus. The Templars were able to defend themselves, and there were even instances when the courts could find no evidence of heresy. Unfortunately, the damage had been done. The lands and other assets of the Templars were eventually redistributed to others.

The End of Jacques de Molay

Grand Master Jacques de Molay was an old man when all of this happened. However, his age did not stop anyone from torturing the elderly knight. He was forced to confess on October 24th, 1307, to all the charges trumped up against him. However, on November 22nd, 1307, the grand master retracted his confessions.

It was an extraordinary act of courage worthy of a knight. But regrettably, it sealed his doom.

On March 18th, 1314, de Molay and three other high-ranking Templars were brought to a podium before Notre-Dame Cathedral. There, they were all publicly condemned to perpetual imprisonment. The grand master and his comrade, Geoffroi de Charney, once again declared their innocence, saying that the Templars were not guilty of the false charges presented against them.

Word of this reached the French king. By then, Philip IV was tired of all the legal trappings. He ordered the three recalcitrant Templars to be burned immediately. On that same day, those three men were burned at the stake in front of the cathedral. An eyewitness recorded these last words of Jacques de Molay, "God knows who is in the wrong and has sinned. Misfortune will soon befall those who have wrongly condemned us; God will avenge our deaths. Make no mistake, all who are against us will suffer because of us. I beseech you to turn my face towards the Virgin Mary, of whom our Lord Christ was born."

The grand master perished, exhibiting the same bravery he expected of any Knight Templar on the battlefield.[57]

---

[57] Selwood, D. (2014, March 18). *A Stain on History: The Burning of Jacques De Molay, Grand Master of the Mysterious Knights Templar, 700 Years Ago Today*. Retrieved from

The Chinon Parchment

The trial and tragedy of the Templars have been discussed for centuries after the order's fall from grace. Theories and speculation have abounded from the chairs of historians throughout the ages. There was discussion that the Vatican deliberately hid the trial documents deep within the bowels of its library. That might not have been the real reason for the disappearance of these documents. It might have been a librarian's mistake.

In 2001, Vatican archivist Barbara Frale made an astounding discovery. Primary documents of the trial were uncovered accidentally. The minutes of the trial, *Processus Contra Templarios*, were published in 2007 by the Vatican, and the papers give tantalizing insights into what happened. The documents do not exonerate the Templars but do something else that is just as important.

The Chinon Parchment is the centerpiece of the material. It suggests that Clement V agonized over what to do with the Templars. The pope was being pressured by Philip IV and did not appreciate having his arm twisted by the French king. The uncovered evidence sheds light on some of the more interesting elements of the case.

Spitting on the crucifix was part of the initiation rite for the Templars. It was not an act of satanic worship. The Templars had to anticipate the possibility of being captured alive by the Muslims. Any effort to break the will of a captured knight might include acts of sacrilege. The trauma of spitting on the cross could be lessened because the captive knight was already involved in this act. However, the initiation rite was not sacrilegious, and spitting on the cross was intended to strengthen the knight's resolve.[58]

Templars were accused of worshiping a head as part of their secret ceremonies. Frale objects to the argument that it was a pagan act. On the contrary, she argues this was a veneration of Jesus. She believes it represented Christ as much as a cross above a Catholic altar represents

---

https://www.dominicselwood.com/my-journalism/a-stain-on-history-the-burning-of-jacques-de-molay-grand-master-of-the-mysterious-knights-templar-700-years-ago-today/; https://www.dominicselwood.com/my-journalism/a-stain-on-history-the-burning-of-jacques-de-molay-grand-master-of-the-mysterious-knights-templar-700-years-ago-today/.

[58] McMahon, T. (2018, July 3). *The Chinon Parchment-A Papal Exoneration of the Knights Templar?* Retrieved from thetemplarknight.com: https://thetemplarknight.com/2018/07/03/chinon-parchment-knights-templar-exoneration/.

the crucifixion. No disrespect was ever intended.

A Compelling "What If?"

History fans love to speculate about what might have happened if events happened differently. We can take a look at the Knights Templar and ask what might have happened if it had not been railroaded by Philip IV and disbanded by Clement V. We would like to take this opportunity to offer our own opinions in the interest of provoking stimulating conversations.

Jacques de Molay wanted to plan another crusade but was arrested before he could do that. A traditional crusade would have been challenging to organize because of a lack of interest. Nevertheless, de Molay could have used an innovative strategy to break the Mamluks and possibly restore the Kingdom of Jerusalem. It would not have required the spilling of Christian blood. It would not have been about swords and arrows. Instead, it would have been about money.

The Knights Templar was a financial juggernaut at the start of the 14th century. There was nothing like its financial network in Western civilization. Templar branches were everywhere, and the knights had their own fleet of ships. They did not need soldiers to attack the Mamluks. Instead of a traditional battlefield, the action could be shifted to the safe counting rooms within the commanderies.

The loss of the Holy Land meant the Templars no longer had to worry about the upkeep of castles and fortresses in Outremer. Freedom from that responsibility would have released a large amount of cash, and those funds would have been at the disposal of the grand master. So, how might this hoard of gold be used? One possible answer lay in Constantinople, where money had been used effectively in the past.

The Byzantines used their treasure to cause trouble in the Islamic world. Evidence shows they paid various desert tribes to stir up trouble behind the lines. This forced the caliphs and sultans to deal with internal issues, distracting them from trying to take chunks of the Byzantine Empire. The Templars could have used the same tactic.

The Muslim world was not a united front. Even today, Shia and Sunni Muslims bicker and quarrel. The Templars could have played one side against the other. It just required helping one party by financing their military efforts. The Mamluks would have to deal with insurgents and could not effectively counter any Christian incursion.

The Templars could go one step further by actively bribing Mamluk generals and pretenders to the sultan's throne. A rash of civil wars would weaken their Muslim enemy. Best of all, the Templars were in no physical danger. They were not in Palestine but in Europe. Any money could be shipped to the right place on a Templar vessel. A Mamluk attack on Europe would not be easy, especially if there were rebels causing trouble in the rear.

The Templars could have also negotiated a return of Acre or even Jerusalem itself in exchange for stopping the flow of money to internal enemies. It would be hard to refuse. The Templars had the wherewithal in Europe to raise money quickly and efficiently and get it to the right place. It was a type of warfare the Mamluks were not accustomed to fighting. Funding insurgencies and shameless bribery might have worked.

Of course, this is all speculation. It is possible that if the Templars had survived, they could have become something comparable to the European Central Bank. Their financial resources could have funded a commercial Renaissance in Europe. All the pieces of that puzzle were there waiting to be put together. Sadly, it did not happen. The Templars were finally bullied and tortured into oblivion. Shortly after they were officially disbanded, they became not much more than a memory.

Chapter Twelve – Legends and Myths

"Non nobis domine, non nobis, sed nomini tuo da gloriam." ("Not to us, Lord, not to us, but give glory to your name.")

-Motto of the Knights Templar

Some fraternal organizations recognize the trappings and terminology of the Templars, but the order itself has been gone for over seven hundred years. Nevertheless, people are still fascinated by these knights in shining armor. The mystique of and legends about the Templars continue to grab our attention. Stories about the Templars are the stock of many fiction books, and the movies love these characters.

We are not going to spoil anybody's fun by casting shade on this love affair with long-dead warriors. It is fun to read fanciful tales about them, and the Templars have made their way into many conspiracy stories. We think you are going to enjoy some legends of the Templars, so we are going to devote this chapter to the most popular ones.

The Curse of the Grand Master

Jacques de Molay spent the last years of his life being interrogated and tortured as the grand master of the Knights Templar. Finally, he broke down and confessed to the trumped-up charges against the order but retracted his confession later. The last time he protested his innocence, Philip IV had enough of the older man and ordered him to be burned at the stake.

Being burned alive before a crowd is a terrible way to die, but the pyre was constructed so the condemned person would die quickly from smoke inhalation. However, the one built for de Molay was prepared so that it would burn slowly. It was a mistake because as he was being consumed by the flames, the grand master cursed the French king and his descendants, Pope Clement V, and those whose treachery led to his execution. He also declared that God would punish the ruling house of France, the Capetians.

De Molay's execution took place on March 18th, 1314. Pope Clement V died on April 20th, 1314. Philip died on November 29th, 1314. Enguerrand de Marigny, a principal player in the fall of the Templars, perished on April 30th, 1315. The Capetian dynasty lasted until 1328 and was succeeded by the House of Valois.

Circumstantial evidence suggests that de Molay's curse was effective. And that is what superstitious people would claim. However, we need to look at some of the facts. First, the pope was seriously ill at the time of de Molay's execution. It was doubtful that he would be able to survive much longer in the first place. He got his final comeuppance thanks to Dante, who placed the pope in the *Inferno* of the *Divine Comedy* because of his role in starting the Babylonian captivity of the papacy.

Second, Philip IV's reign was a stormy one almost from the beginning. He was undoubtedly under incredible stress as king, and his cardiovascular system was already weak. The standard aristocratic diet was heavy on protein and low on vitamins, which may have contributed to physical deterioration. De Marigny was arrested and hanged for corruption.

The Roman Catholic Church formally apologized in June 2011 for de Molay's death and acknowledged that he was killed on false charges.[59]

The Mystery of the Chapel

Rosslyn Chapel is among the most popular tourist attractions in Scotland. There are several stories and legends about the chapel, and the elaborate carvings found on the walls lead some folks to claim that this is a "Stargate" for extraterrestrials. The carvings are so ornate and elaborate that some people think that mystical codes are etched within the walls.

---

[59] Klimczak, N. (2021, September 18). *The Powerful Curse of Jacques de Molay, the Last Grand Master of Templars.* Retrieved from ancient-origins.net: https://www.ancient-origins.net/history-famous-people/curse-jacques-de-molay-templars-005431.

These tales are part of the fun of visiting Rosslyn Chapel, and one of the best is associated with the Knights Templar.

The story gets pride of place in the novel *The Da Vinci Code.* In spite of the accusations and slanders levied against the order by Philip IV, not everyone in Europe believed the Templars were evil. Scotland was a safe refuge for the survivors of the order, and the Templars still owned land in that kingdom. They could safely hide there until sanity prevailed.

If you read the stories of the Templars, you cannot escape the notion they were insanely rich. You also get the impression that they went around with a lot of wealth with them. The connection with Rosslyn Chapel is that the surviving Templars arrived in Scotland with treasure from Solomon's Temple, which they had brought from the Holy Land.

The legend is that this fantastic treasure is buried somewhere beneath Rosslyn Chapel. Supporters of this story note that there is a hidden chamber and that the chapel has Templar symbols carved into the walls.

It sounds fascinating, but the association of the Templars with Rosslyn Chapel and the fabulous wealth buried somewhere on the grounds do not stand up to the facts. Rosslyn Chapel is a historical place of worship with amazing architecture and stone carvings, not the "X" on a treasure map. Until historians and archaeologists come up with solid evidence of a Templar hoard within the walls of the chapel, this is nothing more than the stuff of best-selling fiction books.[60]

The Enormous, Unfound Templar Treasure

The supposed Templar treasure has generated numerous stories and conspiracy theories; nevertheless, historians and scholars generally consider the legend of fabulous riches to be a myth. There is no evidence that the Templars left behind a trove of riches.

Legend also suggests that the Templar treasures included sacred relics and objects, including the Holy Grail, the Ark of the Covenant, and the True Cross. Other stories hint that the fabled hoard consists of gold, silver, and jewels that the order accumulated during its military campaigns and from its financial holdings. However, there is no solid proof that any significant amount of wealth or treasure was left behind by

[60] Rabbie. (2018, January 26). *5 Things You Never Knew About Rosslyn Chapel.* Retrieved from rabbies.com: https://www.rabbies.com/en/blog/5-things-you-never-knew-about-rosslyn-chapel.

the Knights Templar. There are some reasons why any such treasure has yet to be uncovered.

1. The Templars were disbanded in the early 14th century, and Philip IV and other European monarchs quickly seized much of the order's wealth. Any accumulated treasure could have been confiscated or lost when the order was dissolved.
2. Many places where the Templars are said to have hidden or buried treasure are challenging to access or have been altered over time. If there is buried treasure, it may be buried under a skyscraper.
3. Hunting for treasure is complex and very expensive. It requires considerable research, expertise, and costly equipment. We concede that if any treasure was left behind by the Templars, it has yet to be found because no one has been able to locate it.
4. The legend of Templar riches is just that–nothing more than a legend and rumors. The Templars did acquire enormous amounts of valuable assets during their existence. However, no concrete evidence supports any theory that the Templars left behind a vast treasure just waiting to be discovered.

The Templars and the Temple of Solomon

The Temple Mount in Jerusalem was once the order's headquarters. It is easy to conceive of underground vaults where the knights hid all kinds of valuable things, including sacred relics.

The legends say that the Templars discovered the treasures of Solomon and did excavations under the Temple Mount. The excavations supposedly uncovered hidden chambers and secret tunnels where Solomon hid valuables. The story further suggests that the Knights Templar brought these precious objects back to Europe.

Once again, no concrete evidence suggests that Templars did any excavations under the Temple Mount. Although various groups have conducted excavations at the Temple Mount in the past, this area is not easily accessible. The Israeli government has jurisdiction over the site and tightly regulates all archaeological activity at the Temple Mount. It is doubtful that any significant discoveries could be made without official approval.

A final note is that archaeological excavations were not part of the order's mission. The objective of the warrior monks was to protect pilgrims. They did have access to the Temple Mount at one time, but there is no evidence of the Templars conducting excavations or making noteworthy discoveries at the site.

The Holy Grail

The Knights Templar is also associated with the search for the Holy Grail, the cup that Jesus used at the Last Supper. Although the legend of the Holy Grail has always been a matter of speculation, it has become part of the Templars' image in popular culture.

It is suggested the Templars discovered the Holy Grail while digging under the Temple Mount in Jerusalem. The Templars hid the Grail after they were forced to disband.

Another possibility is that the Holy Grail is not a physical object but a metaphor for spiritual enlightenment. The Templars were known for their mystical beliefs and practices, but as far as cosmic enlightenment, there is nothing to suggest that they achieved it. The Grail remains a mystery, and we may never know for sure if the Knights Templar had any hand in searching for it. Nevertheless, it is a story that catches the imagination of people in Hollywood, and fiction writers find this legend of the Templars irresistible.

The Templars in America

There are legends and conspiracy theories suggesting the Templars colonized North America prior to the arrival of Christopher Columbus. Evidence shows that Viking explorers established a settlement in Newfoundland in the early 11th century. There is no evidence to suggest the Knights Templar had any involvement in the early European exploration of North America.

The Templars had ships; a significant Templar naval base was at La Rochelle, France. There is nothing to suggest they went beyond Ireland. Some stories suggest that Templars, who were fleeing their accusers, set sail for North America. There are two problems with this. To begin with, the arrests of the knights were so complete that few, if any, in France escaped.

If they managed to dodge the French authorities looking for them, it makes more sense that they would have fled to England or Scotland, countries that were friendly to the order, than to try to run to an unknown land.

Finally, the Templars were primarily focused on protecting Christian interests in the Levant and Europe. Just as we have no record of the Templars engaging in archaeology or excavations of any sort, there is nothing to indicate they were maritime explorers looking for new lands. The idea of the Templars in North America is an exciting tale, but there is no evidence to suggest that any of them saw the continent.

The Templars and Oak Island

Another theory suggests that the Knights Templar buried treasure on Oak Island, Nova Scotia, in the 14th century. As a result, Oak Island has gained a great deal of attention, particularly on cable TV.

The mystery of Oak Island is centered on a deep pit or shaft that was discovered on the island in the late 18th century. Treasure hunters and excavation teams over the years have attempted to uncover possible treasure but still have yet to find evidence that there is any. Templars are not the only ones connected with Oak Island. Some people believe that Captain Kidd or some other pirate deposited their loot on Oak Island, intending to return for it later.

One of the earliest and most persistent theories about Oak Island and its treasure is that the Knights Templar buried some of the riches on the island. Those who believe this theory point to supposed similarities between markings and symbols found on Oak Island and images associated with the Knights Templar.

Some researchers claim a carving found on a rock near the pit resembles the coat of arms of La Rochelle. Others suggest the design of the pit is the blueprint of medieval fortifications designed by the Templars.

Nevertheless, there is scant evidence that substantiates any of these claims. Instead, experts believe that the Oak Island mystery is more likely a product of legend exaggeration than a historical event. Some go as far as to suggest that it is nothing more than a natural feature of the island, and what looks to be manmade evidence are the remains of earlier attempts made by excavation teams.

Nothing credible supports the Knights Templar ever being on Oak Island. Theories are nice to speculate over, but no tangible evidence supports the idea of Templar treasure there.

The Templars and the Masonic Orders

This story is more interesting because there is some connection between the Templars and the Freemasons. However, the exact nature of this association is a question of debate.

Historically, the Freemasons originated approximately four hundred years ago in Scotland and England. They trace their roots back to stonemason guilds of the Middle Ages and use rituals and symbols found in medieval stonework architecture.

The Templars may have passed their knowledge and traditions to the stonemason guilds in Europe. To expand on this notion, the Templars may have survived as a secret society and passed down their knowledge and practices through the years.

This creates an exciting possibility. Templar sergeants were not always combat troops. Many of them were trained in trade skills, such as carpentry, and stone masonry may have been an occupation for some of the black brothers. When the order was formally disbanded, those Templars who were not imprisoned needed some way to protect themselves. They may have blended into the workforce of Europe, particularly in the construction of cathedrals. Templars might have shared some of their beliefs with the Stonemasons.

It is possible, but many historians say that it is not probable. Conspiracy theories and idle speculation might embellish the association between Stonemasons and the Templars. There is little evidence to suggest that there was shared knowledge. The Freemasons may have looked to the Templars as examples of virtue and courage and little more than that.

The Knights Templar Possessed Mystical Powers

This notion takes us on a detour into the realm of fantasy. Some suggest the Templars were the protectors of secret knowledge that was known only to few. The story speculates that this information was passed down to Freemasons and other Masonic orders. The legend goes further and accuses the Templars of being involved in secret rituals that may have been satanic. One conspiracy theory postulates that the Knights Templar participated in a plot to overthrow the Roman Catholic Church and establish a new world order.

Going even further into the mists of myth, stories insist that the Templars had supernatural powers. For example, they possessed the ability to fly and had the power of invisibility. They might have even been in league with Satan!

If any of this sounds familiar, some of these ideas were part and parcel of the accusations thrown against the Templars in the 14th century. The agents of Philip IV tried to connect the order with the supernatural or the diabolical to convince people that the Templars were heretics and an evil group of men. These claims were reinforced by confessions made by Templars, who, as we mentioned above, were coerced into confessing.

Any admission made by a member of the order resulted from torture. The extent of the physical abuse inflicted on Templars bordered on sadism. However, torture was an accepted criminal justice practice in the Middle Ages. The Templars gave confessions to avoid any further pain.

A common thread that runs through these stories is a lack of evidence. Conspiracy theorists love to ask questions and provide little proof to support their statements. Some of these ideas might be entertaining for evening discussions and nothing more. Still, there may come a day when some text is discovered in the archives of a Vatican palace or windswept monastery that substantiates one of the legends attributed to the Templars. Until then, the tales of these warrior monks are interwoven with fiction.

The proven history of the Templars and their impact are far more impressive than any romantic fairytale. Moreover, the order's contribution to Europe had an influence that lasted long after the last Templar died. Europe in the 12th century was the backwater of the known world. Its presence in the historical record was overshadowed by the achievements in the Islamic world and China. The Crusades opened Europe to the world, and the Templars helped the continent get through the door.

The financial legacy of the Templars is amazing. Their ideas of credit and loans were practically unheard of anywhere else in the world. The Templars created banking practices that were later copied and refined by European bankers, such as the Medici and the Fuggers. The flow of capital, not gunpowder, eventually made Europe a predominant part of the world.

One can only imagine what might have happened had the Templar financial network been permitted to remain intact. One possible comparison would be the invention of the printing press. Once

Gutenberg refined the technology, printing spread like wildfire over Europe and allowed numerous technical and scientific ideas to be shared. Simply put, the Templars would have provided the money to finance those discoveries. The Industrial Revolution might have begun centuries before it did had Philip IV not been so greedy and shortsighted.

Conclusion

The story and the legends of the Knights Templar are still being told seven hundred years after the order was dissolved. Elements of the Knights Templar include:

- Fraternal organizations. Several fraternal organizations trace their roots back to the Knights Templar, including the Masonic Knights Templar, the Order of the Temple of Solomon, and the sovereign Order of the Knights Templar. These organizations are based on traditions and symbols of the original Knights Templar and promote the values that the original order followed.
- Popular culture. Anyone who has seen the Indiana Jones movies or read Dan Brown's novel *The Da Vinci Code* notices how the Templars are a plot element or a central theme. Using Templars as characters or plöt devices is extremely popular in film, literature, and other forms of media.
- Historical research. The Knights Templar is the subject of ongoing historical research and scholarship. New discoveries and interpretations of historical records continue to shed light on the organization's history and impact on medieval Europe. This is also true of research done on the Near East in the Middle Ages.
- Tourism. The Knights Templar was active in several European countries, and its legacy can still be seen in various historical

sites and landmarks. These sites, such as the Temple Church in London and the Templar castle in Tomar, Portugal, continue to attract visitors from all over the world. There are tours explicitly designed to highlight major Templar sites.

Why is there such a fascination with these warrior monks? Perhaps one reason is how closely they tried to follow the principles of an ideal knight. Most medieval knights were nowhere near the image created by troubadours and the romantic novels of the time. Many were barely more than hitmen for the local aristocracy.

The Knights Templar had a mission and a set of standards that molded their behavior and their outlook on life. There is little evidence to suggest that individual Templars profited from the order's enormous wealth. Instead, it appears that they took their vows of poverty seriously. They created a standard that was difficult to follow but not impossible.

We are also fascinated by the mystery surrounding the Templars. There were secret ceremonies the uninitiated did not know about but were speculated on throughout the ages. We might never know all of the traditions and rituals of the Templars. So much remains a secret.

Despite that, the Templars remain a popular subject of conversation, research, and intellectual curiosity. This is because they were a potent military force and financial power in the Middle Ages. Interest in these knights is ongoing, and they will remain famous examples of an age that disappeared centuries ago.

Here's another book by Captivating History that you might like

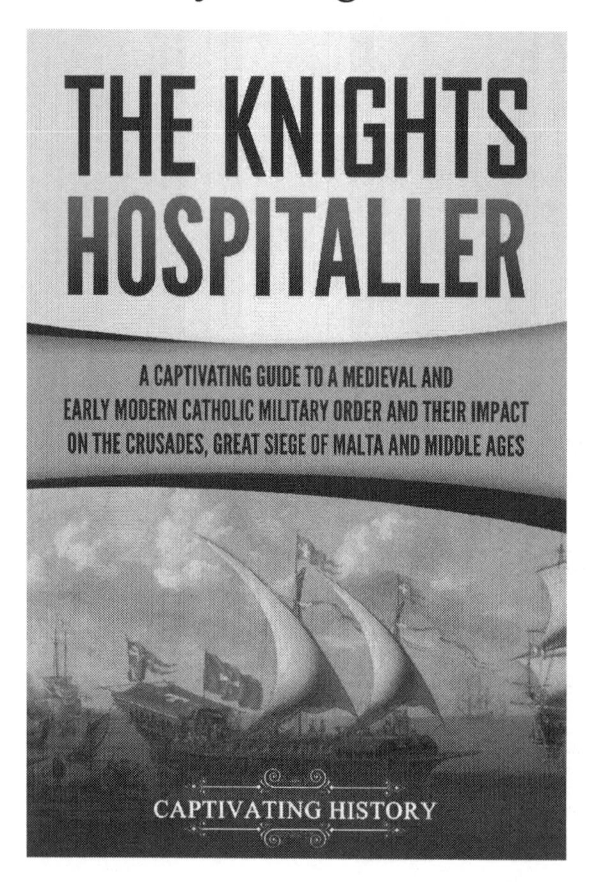

Free Bonus from Captivating History (Available for a Limited time)

Hi History Lovers!

Now you have a chance to join our exclusive history list so you can get your first history ebook for free as well as discounts and a potential to get more history books for free! Simply visit the link below to join.

Captivatinghistory.com/ebook

Also, make sure to follow us on Facebook, Twitter and Youtube by searching for Captivating History.

Bibliography

Ballandalus.com. (2014, February 1). Conquest if Antioch (1268): Letter of Baybars (d.1277) to Bohemond VI (d.1275). Retrieved from ballandalus.wordpress.com: HYPERLINK "https://ballandalus.wordpress.com/2014/02/01/conquest-of-antioch-1268-letter-of-baybars-d-1277-to-bohemond-vi-d-1275/" https://ballandalus.wordpress.com/2014/02/01/conquest-of-antioch-1268-letter-of-baybars-d-1277-to-bohemond-vi-d-1275/

Bevan, R. (2023, February 20). The Templas iIn Iberia: The Reconquista And The Spanish Crusades. Retrieved from history.co.uk: HYPERLINK "https://www.history.co.uk/shows/lost-relics-of-the-knights-templar/articles/the-templars-in-iberia-the-reconquista-and-the" https://www.history.co.uk/shows/lost-relics-of-the-knights-templar/articles/the-templars-in-iberia-the-reconquista-and-the

Bustani, H. A. (2023, February 28). Templar Banking: How to go from Donated Rags to Vast RIches. Retrieved from medievalists.net: HYPERLINK "https://www.medievalists.net/2021/08/templar-banking/" https://www.medievalists.net/2021/08/templar-banking/

Cartwright, M. (2018, September 3). Fourth Crusade. Retrieved from worldhistory.org: HYPERLINK "https://www.worldhistory.org/Fourth_Crusade/" https://www.worldhistory.org/Fourth_Crusade/

Castles.nl. (2023, February 10). San Servando Castle. Retrieved from castles.nl: HYPERLINK "https://www.castles.nl/san-servando-castle" https://www.castles.nl/san-servando-castle

Defenders of Jerusalem.com. (2023, February 2). The Knights Templar Prove their Mettle: The Second Crusade. Retrieved from Defenders of Jerusalem.com: HYPERLINK "https://www.defenderofjerusalem.com/knights-templar---second-crusasde.html" https://www.defenderofjerusalem.com/knights-templar---second-crusasde.html

DefendersofJerusalem.com. (2023, February 28). The Money-Lenders ion the Temple: The Banking Activities of the Knights Templar. Retrieved from defendersofJerusalem.com: HYPERLINK "https://www.defenderofjerusalem.com/templar-banking-activities.html" https://www.defenderofjerusalem.com/templar-banking-activities.html

Dr. Schrader, P. (2921, February 22). The Decline and Fal of the Crusader States in the 13th Century. Retrieved from HYPERLINK "http://defendingcrusaderkingdoms.blogspot.com/" defendingcrusaderkingdoms.blogspot.com : HYPERLINK "http://defendingcrusaderkingdoms.blogspot.com/2021/02/the-decline-and-fall-of-crusader-states.html" http://defendingcrusaderkingdoms.blogspot.com/2021/02/the-decline-and-fall-of-crusader-states.html

Electricscotland.com. (2023, January 31). Bernard of Clairvaux: Patron Saint of the Templar Order. Retrieved from HYPERLINK "https://www.electricscotland.com/" https://www.electricscotland.com/ : HYPERLINK "https://www.electricscotland.com/books/ries/BERNARD%20OF%20CLAIRVAUX%20011713.pdf" https://www.electricscotland.com/books/ries/BERNARD%20OF%20CLAIRVAUX%20011713.pdf

erenow.net. (2023, February 14). Grand Masters 1191-1292/9. Retrieved from erenow.net: HYPERLINK "https://erenow.net/postclassical/the-real-history-behind-the-templars/23.php" https://erenow.net/postclassical/the-real-history-behind-the-templars/23.php

Esq., C. A. (2023, February 15). The Knights Templars. Retrieved from hellenicaworld.com: HYPERLINK "https://www.hellenicaworld.com/History/CGAddison/en/TheKnightsTemplars.html%23CHAPTER_V" https://www.hellenicaworld.com/History/CGAddison/en/TheKnightsTemplars.html#CHAPTER_V

Fascinating Spain. (2023, February 21). Impressive Templar castles in Spain. Retrieved from fascinatingspain.com: HYPERLINK "https://fascinatingspain.com/place-to-visit/the-best-of/impressive-templar-castles-in-spain/" https://fascinatingspain.com/place-to-visit/the-best-of/impressive-templar-castles-in-spain/

Forey, A. (2021, March 18). Early Templar Administration in Provence and North-Eastern Spain. Retrieved from HYPERLINK "https://journals.openedition.org/" journals.openedition.org : HYPERLINK "https://journals.openedition.org/medievalista/4484?lang=en" https://journals.openedition.org/medievalista/4484?lang=en

Gesta Francorum. (1962). Gesta Francorum. In Unknown, Gesta Francorum (p. 93). New York: Oxford University Press.

Harper, I. G. (2023, February 12). The Battle of the Horns of Hattin. Retrieved from northumberlandkt.com: HYPERLINK "https://northumberlandkt.com/?page_id=3874" https://northumberlandkt.com/?page_id=3874

History Crunch.com. (2023, February 18). Fourth Crusade. Retrieved from historycrunch.com: HYPERLINK "https://www.historycrunch.com/fourth-crusade.html" https://www.historycrunch.com/fourth-crusade.html#/

History Learnng.com. (2015, January 1). The Sixth Crusade. Retrieved from historylearning.com: HYPERLINK "https://historylearning.com/medieval-england/the-crusades/sixth-crusade/" https://historylearning.com/medieval-england/the-crusades/sixth-crusade/

History.com. (2021, August 5). Saladin. Retrieved from history.com: HYPERLINK "https://www.history.com/topics/africa/saladin" https://www.history.com/topics/africa/saladin

History-Maps.com. (2023, February 23). 1099-1291 Crusader States (Outremer). Retrieved from history-maps.com: HYPERLINK "https://history-maps.com/story/Crusader-States-Outremer" https://history-maps.com/story/Crusader-States-Outremer

Howe, J. (2016, November/December). Benard's Chosen: The Knights Templar. Retrieved from HYPERLINK "http://myweb.ttu.edu" http://myweb.ttu.edu : HYPERLINK "http://myweb.ttu.edu/jhowe/syllabi/Templar%20Rule.pdf" http://myweb.ttu.edu/jhowe/syllabi/Templar%20Rule.pdf

Imatz, A. (2020, September 1). Al-Andalus: A History Contaminated By Political Correctness. Retrieved from thepostil.com: HYPERLINK "https://www.thepostil.com/al-andalus-a-history-contaminated-by-political-correctness/" https://www.thepostil.com/al-andalus-a-history-contaminated-by-political-correctness/

Jones, D. (2017). The Templars: The Rise and Spectacular Fall Of God's Holy Warriors. New York, NewYork: Penguin Books.

Kannon, C. H. (2023, March 2). King Phillip Iv, Pope Clement V, and the Fall of the Knights Templar. Retrieved from view.officeapps.live.com: HYPERLINK "https://view.officeapps.live.com/op/view.aspx?src=http%3A%2F%2Fplaza.ufl.edu%2Fandrei.gandila%2FPhillip%2520IV_Templars.doc&wdOrigin=BROWSELINK" https://view.officeapps.live.com/op/view.aspx?src=http%3A%2F%2Fplaza.ufl.edu%2Fandrei.gandila%2FPhillip%2520IV_Templars.doc&wdOrigin=BROWSELINK

Klimczak, N. (2021, September 18). The Powerful Curse of Jacques de Molay, the Last Grand Master of Templars. Retrieved from ancient-origins.net: HYPERLINK "https://www.ancient-origins.net/history-famous-people/curse-jacques-de-molay-templars-005431" https://www.ancient-origins.net/history-famous-people/curse-jacques-de-molay-templars-005431

Knightstemplarorder.org. (2023, February 28). Authentic Templar Bankng Principles. Original Biblical Banking Practices of the Knights Templar. Retrieved from knightstemplar.org: HYPERLINK "https://knightstemplarorder.org/heritage/templar-banking/" https://knightstemplarorder.org/heritage/templar-banking/

Knightstemplarvault.com. (2023, March 3). Medieval torture methods applied to the Knights Templar. Retrieved from knightstemplarvault.com: HYPERLINK "https://knightstemplarvault.com/medieval-torture/" https://knightstemplarvault.com/medieval-torture/

Lebling, R. W. (2016, February 1). Arwad, Fortress at Sea. Retrieved from HYPERLINK "https://www.aramcoworld.com/" https://www.aramcoworld.com/ , HYPERLINK "https://www.aramcoworld.com/Articles/January-2016/Arwad-Fortress-at-Sea" https://www.aramcoworld.com/Articles/January-2016/Arwad-Fortress-at-Sea

Lee, J. S. (2022, March 11). The Knights Templar in English Towns. Retrieved from cambridge.org: HYPERLINK "https://www.cambridge.org/core/journals/urban-history/article/knights-templar-in-english-towns/1EB941BD556C016793A6B83499ABC110" https://www.cambridge.org/core/journals/urban-history/article/knights-templar-in-english-towns/1EB941BD556C016793A6B83499ABC110

Lyons, Z. (2023, February 11). Temple Church and the Knights Templar. Retrieved from layersoflondon.org: HYPERLINK "https://www.layersoflondon.org/map/records/temple-church-and-the-knights-templar" https://www.layersoflondon.org/map/records/temple-church-and-the-knights-templar

McMahon, T. (2012, March 27). Temple Mount-HQ of the Knights Templar. Retrieved from thetemplarknight.com: HYPERLINK "https://thetemplarknight.com/2012/03/27/temple-mount-knights-templar/" https://thetemplarknight.com/2012/03/27/temple-mount-knights-templar/

McMahon, T. (2013, December 30). Knights Templar links to the Cathar heresy. Retrieved from thetemplarknight.com: HYPERLINK "https://thetemplarknight.com/2013/12/30/knights-templar-cathars/" https://thetemplarknight.com/2013/12/30/knights-templar-cathars/

McMahon, T. (2017, October 3). Ten Accusations made against the Knights Templar. Retrieved from thetemplarknight.com: HYPERLINK "https://thetemplarknight.com/2017/10/03/knights-templar-accusations/" https://thetemplarknight.com/2017/10/03/knights-templar-accusations/

McMahon, T. (2018, July 3). The Chinon parchment-a papal exoneration of the Knights Templar? Retrieved from thetemplarknight.com: HYPERLINK "https://thetemplarknight.com/2018/07/03/chinon-parchment-knights-templar-exoneration/" https://thetemplarknight.com/2018/07/03/chinon-parchment-knights-templar-exoneration/

Medieval Chronicles.com. (2023, February 1). 8 Strange Rules Templar Knights had to Obey? Retrieved from HYPERLINK "https://www.medievalchronicles.com/" https://www.medievalchronicles.com/ : HYPERLINK "https://www.medievalchronicles.com/the-crusades/knights-templar/knights-templar-and-the-latin-rule/" https://www.medievalchronicles.com/the-crusades/knights-templar/knights-templar-and-the-latin-rule/

Medieval Warfare.info. (2023, February 26). Monastic Orders Kinghts Templar, Knightys Hospitaller and others. Retrieved from medievalwarfare.info: HYPERLINK "https://www.medievalwarfare.info/templars.htm" \l ":~:text=Sergeants.,cavalry%20with%20a%20single%20horse" https://www.medievalwarfare.info/templars.htm#:~:text=Sergeants.,cavalry%20with%20a%20single%20horse .

Meyer, J. R. (2023, January 1). St. Bernard of Clairvaux. Retrieved from www.Britannica.com: HYPERLINK "https://www.britannica.com/biography/Saint-Bernard-of-Clairvaux" https://www.britannica.com/biography/Saint-Bernard-of-Clairvaux

My Travels in the Levant. (2023, February 10). Tartous and Arwad. Retrieved from HYPERLINK "https://romeartlover.tripod.com/" https://romeartlover.tripod.com : HYPERLINK "https://romeartlover.tripod.com/Tortosa.html" https://romeartlover.tripod.com/Tortosa.html

Napier, G. (2016, April 21). Templars, Cathars, and Mary Magdalene (part 1). Retrieved from gordonnapierhistory.blogspot.com: HYPERLINK "http://gordonnapierhistory.blogspot.com/2010/04/templars-cathars-and-mary-magdalene.html" http://gordonnapierhistory.blogspot.com/2010/04/templars-cathars-and-mary-magdalene.html

Nicholson, H. J. (2003, May 1). The Motivations of the Templars in Their Involvment in the Fourth Crusade and its aftermath. Retrieved from researchgate.net: HYPERLINK "https://www.researchgate.net/publication/264646303_The_Motivations_of_the_Hospitallers_and_Templars_in_their_involvement_in_the_Fourth_Crusade_and_its_aftermath" https://www.researchgate.net/publication/264646303_The_Motivations_of_the_Hospitallers_and_Templars_in_their_involvement_in_the_Fourth_Crusade_and_its_aftermath

Ofteland. (2016, July 1). La Rochelle-Atlantic Ocean Base for the Knights Templar. Retrieved from discoversecretfrancecom.wordpress.com: HYPERLINK "https://discoversecretfrancedotcom.wordpress.com/2016/07/14/la-rochelle-atlantic-ocean-base-for-the-knights-templar/" https://discoversecretfrancedotcom.wordpress.com/2016/07/14/la-rochelle-atlantic-ocean-base-for-the-knights-templar/

Pius XII, P. (1953, May 24). On St. Bernard of Claoirvaux, the Last of the Fathers. Retrieved from HYPERLINK "https://www.ewtn.com/" https://www.ewtn.com/ : HYPERLINK "https://www.ewtn.com/catholicism/library/on-st-bernard-of-clairvaux-the-last-of-the-fathers-3537" https://www.ewtn.com/catholicism/library/on-st-bernard-of-clairvaux-the-last-of-the-fathers-3537

Prester John. (2021, September 4). Prester John 3: The Fifth Crusade.

Rabbie. (2018, January 26). 5 Things You Never Knew About Rosslyn Chapel. Retrieved from rabbies.com: HYPERLINK "https://www.rabbies.com/en/blog/5-things-you-never-knew-about-rosslyn-chapel" https://www.rabbies.com/en/blog/5-things-you-never-knew-about-rosslyn-chapel

Schrader, H. P. (2023, February 24). THe Knights Templar and the Fall of Acre 1291. Retrieved from defenderofjerusalem.com: HYPERLINK "https://www.defenderofjerusalem.com/kt---acre.html" https://www.defenderofjerusalem.com/kt---acre.html

Selwood, D. (2014, March 18). A Stain on History: The Burning of Jacques De Molay, Grand Master of the MysteriousKnights Templar, 700 Years ago today. Retrieved from HYPERLINK "https://www.dominicselwood.com/my-journalism/a-stain-on-history-the-burning-of-jacques-de-molay-grand-master-of-the-mysterious-knights-templar-700-years-ago-today/" https://www.dominicselwood.com/my-journalism/a-stain-on-history-the-burning-of-jacques-de-molay-grand-master-of-the-mysterious-knights-templar-700-years-ago-today/ : HYPERLINK " https://www.dominicselwood.com/my-journalism/a-stain-on-history-the-burning-of-jacques-de-molay-grand-master-of-the-mysterious-knights-templar-700-years-ago-today/" https://www.dominicselwood.com/my-journalism/a-stain-on-history-the-burning-of-jacques-de-molay-grand-master-of-the-mysterious-knights-templar-700-years-ago-today/

Slavin, P. (2014, February 19). The Templars' Land. Retrieved from medieval.eu: HYPERLINK "https://www.medieval.eu/knights-templars-land/" https://www.medieval.eu/knights-templars-land/

Stables, D. (2021, October 3). On the trail of the Knights Templar on Portugal. Retrieved from roughguides.com

Suhr, R. (2023, February 12). Crusader Crucible: The Horns of Hattin. Retrieved from HYPERLINK "warfarehistorynetwork.com:%20https://warfarehistorynetwork.com/crusader-crucible-the-horns-of-hattin/" warfarehistorynetwork.com: https://warfarehistorynetwork.com/crusader-crucible-the-horns-of-hattin/

Tax Fitness.com. (2008, January 23). 1188-Saladin Tithe: One of the First Recorded Taxes on Income. Retrieved from taxftness.com.au: HYPERLINK "https://taxfitness.com.au/Blog/1188-saladin-tithe" https://taxfitness.com.au/Blog/1188-saladin-tithe

Templar History. (2020, June 7). Hugues dr Payens-The First Grand Master. Retrieved from https: templarhistory.com: HYPERLINK "https://templarhistory.com/hugues-de-payens-the-first-grand-master/" https://templarhistory.com/hugues-de-payens-the-first-grand-master/

Templars-route.eu. (2023, February 26). Templar Heritage in France. Retrieved from templars-route.eu: HYPERLINK "https://www.templars-route.eu/en/templar-heritage-in-france/" https://www.templars-route.eu/en/templar-heritage-in-france/

The Crusader Kingdoms. (2023, January 30). Luxury Exports and Religious Tourist: The Urban Economy of Outremer. Retrieved from HYPERLINK "https://www.crusaderkingdoms.com/" https://www.crusaderkingdoms.com/ : HYPERLINK "https://www.crusaderkingdoms.com/urban-economy.html" https://www.crusaderkingdoms.com/urban-economy.html

ThoughtCo.com. (2023, February 15). The Battle of Arsuf in the Crusades. Retrieved from thoughtco.com: HYPERLINK "https://www.thoughtco.com/the-crusades-battle-of-arsuf-2360710" https://www.thoughtco.com/the-crusades-battle-of-arsuf-2360710

Timenote.info. (2023, February 23). First Mongk Invasion of Poland; Battle of Legnica. Retrieved from timenote.info: HYPERLINK "https://timenote.info/en/events/First-Mongol-invasion-of-Poland-Battle-of-Legnica" https://timenote.info/en/events/First-Mongol-invasion-of-Poland-Battle-of-Legnica

Tourist Israel. (2023, February 10). The Templar's Tunnel, Akko (Acre). Retrieved from www.touristisrael.com: HYPERLINK "https://www.touristisrael.com/templars-tunnel-akko/28509/" https://www.touristisrael.com/templars-tunnel-akko/28509/

Turney, S. (2020, July 25). The Templars and the reconquest of Spain. Retrieved from historiamag.com: HYPERLINK "https://www.historiamag.com/templars-and-the-reconquest-of-spain/" https://www.historiamag.com/templars-and-the-reconquest-of-spain/

Walker, J. (2023, February 14). Soldiers of God. Retrieved from warfarehistorynetwork.com: HYPERLINK "https://warfarehistorynetwork.com/article/saldains-defeat-at-the-hands-of-the-knights-templar/" https://warfarehistorynetwork.com/article/saldains-defeat-at-the-hands-of-the-knights-templar/

Watson, C. C. (2023, February 20). The Battle of Las Navas de Tolosa. Retrieved from andalucia.com: HYPERLINK "https://www.andalucia.com/spainsmoorishhistory/las-navas-de-tolosa.htm" https://www.andalucia.com/spainsmoorishhistory/las-navas-de-tolosa.htm

Welton, B. (2016, August 16). 10 Overlooked Facts About The Spanish Reconquest. Retrieved from listverse.com: HYPERLINK "https://listverse.com/2016/08/16/10-overlooked-facts-about-the-spanish-reconquest/" https://listverse.com/2016/08/16/10-overlooked-facts-about-the-spanish-reconquest/

Wikipedia.com. (2023, February 10). Castle of Almourol. Retrieved from en.wikipedia.org/wiki: HYPERLINK "https://en.wikipedia.org/wiki/Castle_of_Almourol" https://en.wikipedia.org/wiki/Castle_of_Almourol

Wikipedia.com. (2023, February 10). Chateau Pelerin. Retrieved from HYPERLINK "https://en.wikipedia.org/wiki:%20https:/en.wikipedia.org/wiki/Ch%C3%A2teau_P%C3%A8lerin" https://en.wikipedia.org/wiki: https://en.wikipedia.org/wiki/Ch%C3%A2teau_P%C3%A8lerin

Wikipedia.com. (2023, February 18). Fifth Crusade. Retrieved from en.wikipedia.org/wiki: HYPERLINK "https://en.wikipedia.org/wiki/Fifth_Crusade" https://en.wikipedia.org/wiki/Fifth_Crusade

Wikipedia.com. (2023, February 10). Peniscola Castle. Retrieved from en.wikipedia.org/wiki: HYPERLINK "https://en.wikipedia.org/wiki/Peniscola_Castle" https://en.wikipedia.org/wiki/Peniscola_Castle

Wikipedia.com. (2023, February 22). Siege of Alcacer do Sol. Retrieved from en.wikipedia.org/wiki: HYPERLINK "https://en.wikipedia.org/wiki/Siege_of_Alc%C3%A1cer_do_Sal" https://en.wikipedia.org/wiki/Siege_of_Alc%C3%A1cer_do_Sal

Wikipedia.com. (2023, February 18). Siege of Damietta (1218-1219). HYPERLINK "https://en.wikipedia.org/wiki/Siege_of_Damietta_(1218%E2%80%931219)" https://en.wikipedia.org/wiki/Siege_of_Damietta_(1218%E2%80%931219) , p. 1.

Wikipedia.org. (2023, March 2). Trials of the Knights Templar. Retrieved from en.wikipedia.org: HYPERLINK "https://en.wikipedia.org/wiki/Trials_of_the_Knights_Templar" https://en.wikipedia.org/wiki/Trials_of_the_Knights_Templar

Wikiwand.com. (2023, March 4). Council of Vienne. Retrieved from wikiwand.com: HYPERLINK "https://www.wikiwand.com/en/Council_of_Vienne" https://www.wikiwand.com/en/Council_of_Vienne

Wilipedia.com. (2023, January 30). Crusader states. HYPERLINK "https://en.wikipedia.org/wiki/Crusader_states" https://en.wikipedia.org/wiki/Crusader_states , p. 1.

HYPERLINK "https://www.portugaltravel.org/" https://www.portugaltravel.org/ . (2023, February 10). Castle of the Knights Templar in Tomar. Retrieved from portugaltravel.org: HYPERLINK "https://www.portugaltravel.org/castle-of-the-knihgts-templar-tomar" https://www.portugaltravel.org/castle-of-the-knihgts-templar-tomar

Made in the USA
Monee, IL
08 May 2024